Visionary Pathways
A Teen's Quest for Leadership in the Technological Era

Table of Contents

Foreword

In "Visionary Pathways: A Teen's Quest for Leadership in the Technological Era," I embark on an introspective journey, chronicling my experiences as a young innovator navigating the complex world of technology, leadership, and community service. As a high school student standing on the precipice of college and the vast unknowns of the future, this book is more than a mere compilation of achievements; it's a testament to the power of youthful curiosity and the impact of visionary leadership.

From the very beginning, my path has been anything but conventional. Drawn to the enigmatic realms of quantum computing and robotics, I plunged into these fields with a zeal that transcended the typical boundaries of high school education. My passion for these subjects was not fueled solely by a thirst for knowledge but also by a deep-seated desire to use technology as a tool for positive societal change. This book is a narrative of that journey, encapsulating my efforts to democratize technology and education through initiatives like the Rohbot Kit and illuminEd Inc.

Yet, this is not just a story about technological pursuits. It's about the human element in innovation—the triumphs, the setbacks, and the invaluable lessons learned along the way. It's about the mentors who guided me, the peers who inspired me, and the communities that shaped my perspective on leadership and social responsibility.

As I stand at the crossroads of high school and higher education, I am keenly aware that the path I have chosen is uncharted and challenging. However, it's a path I embrace with optimism and determination. This book, therefore, is not just a reflection of my past but also a blueprint for my future aspirations.

To my fellow students, mentors, and anyone embarking on their own journey of discovery and leadership, I hope this book serves as a beacon, encouraging you to pursue your passions, no matter how daunting they may seem. For in the words of the great quantum physicist Niels Bohr, "An expert is a person who has made all the mistakes that can be made in a very narrow field." As you will see in the chapters that follow, my journey is filled with both mistakes and milestones, each shaping the leader I aspire to become.

Welcome to "Visionary Pathways," a narrative of relentless curiosity, unwavering ambition, and the transformative power of youthful leadership.

Sincerely,

Rohan Jay

Introduction: The Journey of a Teen Visionary

As I sit down to pen this introduction, I am reminded of a quote by Steve Jobs, "Innovation distinguishes between a leader and a follower." These words have resonated with me throughout my journey as a young innovator. My story is not just about embracing the fields of quantum computing, machine learning, and robotics, but about leading with vision and purpose. It is about using technology not merely as a tool for personal achievement but as a catalyst for positive societal change.

My journey began with an insatiable curiosity and a computer screen glowing with lines of code. From an early age, I was fascinated by the mysteries of technology and the endless possibilities it held. As I ventured deeper into the realms of quantum computing and robotics, I realized that my passion for technology could be harnessed to bridge gaps in education and opportunity. This realization set me on a path that was far from typical for a teenager.

In these pages, you will find stories of my deep dive into the world of quantum computing, where I explored the potential speed-up benefits of quantum transformers in large language models. You will read about the 'Rohbot Kit,' a project born out of my desire to make robotics accessible to underprivileged students without computer access. This project wasn't just about building a kit; it was about opening doors to a world that many students never knew existed.

But this book is more than just a collection of achievements. It's a story of the challenges and setbacks that came along with my pursuit of innovation. It's about the nights spent troubleshooting codes, the failures that taught me resilience, and the realization that true leadership involves lifting others as you climb.

As I prepare to embark on the next phase of my journey – college and beyond – I reflect on the lessons learned and the experiences gained. This book is my attempt to share those lessons with others who, like me, are driven by a desire to lead, innovate, and make a meaningful impact in the world.

In these chapters, I will take you through the various facets of my journey - the triumphs, the trials, and the invaluable learnings. From developing technology solutions for social challenges to leading community initiatives, every experience has been a stepping stone in shaping my vision of leadership.

As you turn these pages, I invite you to join me on this journey. Whether you are a student, a mentor, or someone passionate about technology and leadership, I hope my story inspires you to chase your dreams, no matter how ambitious they may seem. For in the heart of a visionary, every challenge is an opportunity, and every dream is a possibility waiting to be realized.

Welcome to my journey – the journey of a teen visionary.

Chapter 1: Early Inspirations

My journey into the world of technology and leadership did not begin in a state-of-the-art laboratory or a high-powered conference room. It started in the modest surroundings of my childhood home, where a curious mind met the boundless potential of a computer.

The Spark of Curiosity

From a very young age, I was intrigued by how things worked. I remember dismantling toys just to see their inner workings, much to my parents' dismay. This inquisitiveness soon found a new outlet: technology. My first encounter with a computer was not just fascinating; it was transformative. It was as if I had discovered a portal to an infinite universe of knowledge and possibilities.

Role Models That Shaped My Path

My early foray into technology was heavily influenced by figures who, to me, epitomized innovation and leadership. Icons like Steve Jobs, Elon Musk, and Marie Curie were not just names in textbooks; they were beacons of inspiration. Their stories of resilience, creativity, and impact taught me that technology was more than circuits and codes; it was a tool for changing the world.

A World of Books and Learning

I was fortunate to have access to a treasure trove of books. From science fiction novels that expanded my imagination to biographies that offered glimpses into the minds of great innovators, these books were my early mentors. They opened my eyes to the power of ideas and the importance of persistence in the face of challenges.

The First Steps into Coding

My actual tryst with technology began with coding. I started with basic programming languages, and the thrill of writing a program that could solve a problem or create something new was exhilarating. This was not just a hobby; it became a passion. I spent hours learning and experimenting, and with each line of code, I felt more empowered to make a difference.

Lessons from Early Failures

Not every project was a success. There were times when my code didn't work, or my ideas fell flat. These moments were tough, but they were also invaluable. They taught me that failure was not the end but a part of the learning process. It was through these failures that I learned the importance of resilience and adaptability – traits that would become cornerstones of my journey.

Embracing the Interdisciplinary Approach

Early on, I realized that technology was not a standalone field; it intersected with everything from art to science to the humanities. This interdisciplinary approach became a guiding principle for me. I sought to learn beyond the confines of conventional education, exploring subjects like physics, mathematics, and even philosophy, understanding that true innovation lies at the crossroads of diverse fields.

The First Milestone: A Small Invention

My first significant project was a simple yet impactful invention. This project was a turning point, marking my transition from a curious learner to a young innovator.

As I reflect on these early inspirations, I realize they laid the foundation for my journey. They instilled in me a love for learning, a passion for technology, and a desire to lead with purpose. This chapter of my life was just the beginning, but its lessons and experiences have been the guiding lights for my path forward.

Chapter 2: Discovering a Passion for Technology

The seeds of my passion for technology were sown in the most unassuming of places: a small, cluttered desk in the corner of my room, illuminated by the soft glow of a computer screen. It was here, amidst a tangle of wires and the rhythmic hum of the machine, that my fascination with the digital world began to take root.

The First Encounter

My journey into the realm of technology began with an old, hand-me-down computer. To many, it might have seemed outdated, but to me, it was a treasure trove of possibilities. The first time I powered it on, I was greeted by a world that was entirely new and captivating. The blinking cursor on the screen was like a gateway to a universe waiting to be explored.

A World Beyond the Screen

As I dug deeper into the workings of the computer, I discovered that technology was not just about what was happening on the screen. It was about understanding the language of machines, deciphering the logic that powered them, and, most importantly, realizing how they could be harnessed to solve real-world problems. This realization was a turning point, transforming my casual interest into a genuine passion.

Learning to Speak 'Code'

My initial entry into programming was both daunting and exhilarating. I started with basic languages like Python and Java, reveling in the joy of creating something from nothing but lines of code. Each program I wrote, whether a simple calculator or a basic game, felt like a personal triumph. It was as if I had learned to speak a new language, one that allowed me to communicate with the digital world.

The Magic of Making and Breaking

I wasn't content with just following instructions; I wanted to experiment, to make and break things. I spent countless hours tinkering with hardware and software, often resulting in a non-functional computer and a slightly frustrated yet amused family. But each mistake was a lesson, and every failure was a step closer to understanding the intricate dance of technology.

The Community of Innovators

As my interest grew, I discovered an entire community of like-minded individuals: forums, online courses, and local tech clubs. Engaging with this community was invigorating. I was no longer a lone explorer but part of a global network of innovators, each sharing, learning, and pushing the boundaries of what was possible with technology.

Realizing Technology's Potential for Impact

Perhaps the most significant moment in my early technological journey was realizing the immense potential technology had for making a positive impact on society. Whether it was reading about the latest breakthroughs in artificial intelligence or seeing how open-source software could empower communities, I understood that technology was a tool for change, a means to make the world a better, more connected place.

In these early stages of my journey, technology was more than a hobby or an academic pursuit; it was a window into the future. It showed me a world where challenges could be met with creativity, where innovation was the key to unlocking new possibilities, and where a young enthusiast like me could dream of making a mark. This was the beginning of a path that would take me to uncharted territories, a path where my passion for technology would become the driving force behind my aspirations and achievements.

Chapter 3: Role Models and Mentors in My Early Years

As I navigated the intricacies of technology and leadership, I was fortunate to have a constellation of role models and mentors who illuminated my path. These individuals, each a paragon in their respective fields, provided me with the inspiration and guidance that shaped my early years and carved out the trajectory of my journey.

1. The Tech Visionaries: Inspirations from Afar

My first mentors were the tech visionaries whose stories I devoured in books and online articles. Figures like Steve Jobs, whose relentless pursuit of perfection in design and innovation taught me the value of attention to detail and the power of vision. Elon Musk's audacious goals in space and renewable energy showed me the importance of thinking big and challenging the status quo. Then there was Marie Curie, whose pioneering work in physics and chemistry, despite numerous societal hurdles, was a testament to the resilience and tenacity required in the pursuit of knowledge and innovation.

2. Academic Guides: Teachers and Educators

In the halls of my school, I found mentors in teachers who recognized and nurtured my budding interest in technology. There was Mr. Smith, my computer science teacher, who first introduced me to programming. He saw potential in my clumsy lines of code and encouraged me to dive deeper. Mrs. Davis, my physics teacher, made the world of quantum mechanics come alive in her classes, fueling my fascination with the subject.

3. Community Mentors: Local Tech Enthusiasts

My journey was further enriched by the local community of tech enthusiasts. I remember attending a robotics workshop at a nearby community center, where I met Mr. Lee, an engineer who spent his weekends teaching kids like me. His hands-on approach to teaching and his patience with my endless questions were instrumental in my early robotics projects.

4. Family: The Unsung Heroes

My family played an integral role as silent mentors. My parents, with a strong background in technology, showed me the meaning of unconditional support. They were my sounding board for ideas, my consolation during failures, and my cheerleaders during successes.

5. Online Communities: Global Connectivity

As I dove into the digital world, online communities became a vital source of mentorship. From forums on coding and robotics to online courses by experts in various fields, these platforms allowed me to connect with global experts and peers, broadening my horizons and exposing me to diverse perspectives and ideas.

6. Personal Encounters: Chance Meetings that Inspired

There were also chance encounters that left an indelible mark on my journey. Like the time I met a software developer at a tech fair who spent hours discussing the future of AI with me, or when I had the opportunity to interact with a group of entrepreneurs at a local startup event, their stories of turning ideas into reality further fueled my passion for technology and innovation.

In reflecting on these role models and mentors, I realize they were more than just guides; they were catalysts that sparked my passion, challenged my thinking, and encouraged me to dream bigger. They taught me that while the journey of innovation is often solitary, it is the wisdom, support, and inspiration from those around us that truly propels us forward. As I continue on my path, the lessons learned and the inspiration drawn from these role models and mentors remain a guiding light, shaping the person and innovator I aspire to be.

Chapter 4: Exploring Quantum Mechanics and Computing

Quantum mechanics, an enigma of modern science, was a field I approached with a blend of awe and curiosity. My journey into this realm wasn't just about understanding its principles; it was about exploring how these principles could be harnessed to revolutionize computing. This exploration became a cornerstone in my journey, shaping my understanding of technology's future.

In my early teens, as I dug deeper into the realms of technology, I stumbled upon a field that seemed to defy the very laws of physics as I knew them – quantum computing. This chapter of my life marks the beginning of an enthralling journey into a domain that promised to redefine the future of computing.

The Fascination Begins

My fascination with quantum computing began almost serendipitously. A documentary on quantum physics, watched out of sheer curiosity, opened my eyes to the enigmatic world of quantum mechanics. I was captivated by the principles of superposition and entanglement and their potential applications in computing. It was a world where classical bits transformed into quantum qubits, where computers could process complex calculations at unprecedented speeds.

Self-Taught Quantum Explorer

With no formal courses available in my school curriculum, I embarked on a self-taught journey. Armed with online resources, textbooks, and a burning desire to learn, I began to unravel the complexities of quantum algorithms and quantum circuits. I spent nights poring over scholarly articles, trying to grasp the nuances of this groundbreaking technology.

First Quantum Programming Experiences

My first hands-on experience with quantum computing came when I discovered quantum programming languages like Qiskit. This was a game-changer. I could now write and test quantum algorithms, experiencing the thrill of seeing my theoretical knowledge come to life. My first successful implementation of a simple quantum circuit was a moment of triumph and a glimpse into the potential that lay ahead.

Challenges and Perseverance

The journey was not without its challenges. Quantum computing was a field at the very edge of modern science, complex and often counterintuitive. There were moments of frustration, times when the algorithms I wrote refused to work, or the concepts seemed too abstract to grasp. But with each hurdle, my resolve to master this field only grew stronger.

The Quantum Computing Community

I soon realized that the world of quantum computing was nurtured by a vibrant and supportive community. Online forums, webinars, and virtual workshops became my regular haunts. Interacting with researchers, professionals, and fellow enthusiasts from around the globe, I gained not only knowledge but also a sense of belonging to a community at the forefront of technological innovation.

Envisioning the Future

As I explored further into quantum computing, I began to envision its future applications. From cryptography to drug discovery, from optimizing complex systems to solving problems currently beyond the reach of classical computers – the possibilities were limitless. I dreamed of contributing to this field, of being part of the revolution that would change how we perceive and interact with the world of computing.

My Quantum Projects

My foray into quantum computing led me to initiate several personal projects. These projects were not just academic exercises; they were stepping stones that cemented my passion and commitment to the field of quantum computing.

Quantum computing, with its blend of physics and computer science, was more than just an academic interest; it was a beacon that guided me towards uncharted territories. It represented a new frontier, not just in technology but in my personal journey of exploration and discovery. As I look back on this chapter, it stands as a testament to my growth as a learner, a thinker, and a visionary, poised at the edge of tomorrow's technology.

Unraveling the Mysteries of Quantum Mechanics

My initial encounter with quantum mechanics was akin to stepping into a new universe. Concepts like wave-particle duality, superposition, and entanglement seemed more like science fiction than reality. As I dived into the works of pioneers like Niels Bohr, Werner Heisenberg, and Erwin Schrödinger, I realized that these concepts were not just theoretical abstractions but underpinned the very fabric of our universe. Grasping these ideas was challenging yet exhilarating.

The Quantum-Computing Connection

The leap from understanding quantum mechanics to quantum computing was a thrilling transition. Quantum computing promised to leverage the strange behavior of particles at the quantum level to perform computations that were beyond the scope of classical computing. This meant dealing with qubits (quantum bits) that, unlike traditional bits, could exist in multiple states simultaneously, thanks to superposition.

Simulating Quantum Phenomena

Armed with a foundational understanding of quantum mechanics, I began experimenting with quantum simulations. Tools like IBM's Quantum Experience provided a platform to create and test quantum circuits. Designing these circuits was not just programming; it was like choreographing a dance of particles, each step unlocking new computational possibilities.

The Challenge of Quantum Algorithms

Quantum algorithms were a realm unto themselves. Algorithms like Shor's for factoring large numbers and Grover's for database search operations opened my eyes to the sheer power of quantum computing. Yet, understanding and implementing these algorithms required a deep conceptual shift from classical computing methods. The more I learned, the more I appreciated the elegance and complexity of these algorithms.

Quantum Entanglement: A Puzzling Phenomenon

One of the most fascinating aspects of quantum mechanics I explored was entanglement. This phenomenon, where particles become interconnected and the state of one instantly influences the other, regardless of distance, was mind-bending. Entanglement not only challenged my understanding of physics but also hinted at the potential for revolutionary new forms of communication and computing.

Practical Applications: From Theory to Reality

As my knowledge deepened, I began to explore the practical applications of quantum computing. From its potential to solve complex optimization problems to its ability to disrupt current cryptographic methods, the implications were vast. I was particularly intrigued by the potential for quantum computing in areas like drug discovery and materials science, where it could simulate molecular interactions with unprecedented accuracy.

Philosophical Implications and Ethical Considerations

My exploration of quantum mechanics and computing also led me to ponder its philosophical and ethical implications. The probabilistic nature of quantum mechanics challenged classical notions of determinism, while the power of quantum computing raised questions about privacy, security, and the future of work in a quantum-powered world.

In exploring quantum mechanics and computing, I didn't just gain knowledge; I gained a new perspective on the potential of science and technology. It was a journey that took me to the frontiers of human understanding, a journey where every discovery was a step into a future brimming with possibilities. This exploration was not just about acquiring skills or understanding concepts; it was about preparing myself for a future where quantum computing would redefine the boundaries of what is possible.

Chapter 5: My First Steps into Quantum Research

Embarking on a journey into quantum research as a high school student was both daunting and exhilarating. It represented my transition from a curious learner to an active participant in a field that stood at the cutting edge of science and technology. This chapter of my life was about taking the theoretical knowledge I had gathered and applying it to real-world problems, marking my first foray into the realm of quantum research.

The Genesis of My Quantum Research Journey

My quantum research journey began with a simple yet profound question: "How can the principles of quantum mechanics be applied to solve complex problems?" This question was the seed from which my research aspirations grew. I knew that to find answers, I had to dig deeper, beyond textbooks and simulations, into the realm of practical application.

Choosing a Research Focus

Deciding on a focus for my research was a critical step. After much deliberation, I settled on the area of quantum algorithms. I was fascinated by the potential of these algorithms to process information in ways that were impossible for classical computers. My goal was to explore the development of a quantum algorithm that could address a specific problem in computational science.

Crafting the Research Proposal

Writing a research proposal was my first challenge. I had to articulate my ideas clearly and convincingly, outlining the objectives, methodology, and potential impact of my research. This process honed my skills in critical thinking and scientific writing. I learned to transform a nebulous idea into a structured research plan.

Finding a Mentor

Recognizing the need for guidance, I sought a mentor in the field. After numerous emails and meetings, I connected with Dr. Alan Thompson, a quantum physicist at a local university. Dr. Thompson's expertise in quantum computing and his willingness to guide a high school student was invaluable. He provided insights that deepened my understanding and challenged me to think more critically about my work.

The Learning Curve

The initial stages of my research were steeped in learning and experimentation. I spent hours in the university lab, familiarizing myself with quantum computing platforms and experimenting with different quantum algorithms. This hands-on experience was integral to my growth as a young researcher.

Overcoming Obstacles

My research journey was not without obstacles. There were moments of frustration when experiments didn't go as planned or when concepts seemed too complex to grasp. But these challenges were also opportunities for learning. With each setback, I learned the value of perseverance and the importance of a methodical approach to problem-solving.

Presenting My Findings

The culmination of my initial research efforts was presenting my findings. I prepared a paper and presented it at a local science fair. The experience of sharing my work, answering questions, and receiving feedback was both nerve-wracking and exhilarating. It was a validation of my efforts and a glimpse into the collaborative nature of scientific research.

Reflecting on the Journey

Looking back on my first steps into quantum research, I see more than just a scientific endeavor. It was a journey of personal growth. I learned to navigate the complexities of research, to communicate my ideas effectively, and to collaborate with others in the scientific community. This experience was a foundational step in my journey as a young scientist, setting the stage for more advanced research and exploration in the field of quantum computing.

In this chapter of my life, I learned that research is more than just a pursuit of knowledge; it's a commitment to pushing the boundaries of what we know and what we can achieve. My first steps into quantum research were just the beginning, but they were crucial in shaping my path towards becoming a contributor to this exciting and rapidly evolving field.

Chapter 6: Developing the Rohbot Kit: A Story of Innovation

The story of the Rohbot Kit is one of innovation, driven by a vision to democratize access to robotics education. This journey was not just about creating a product; it was about challenging the status quo and bridging the gap between advanced technology and accessible learning tools.

My journey into the world of robotics began not in a classroom or a lab, but from a desire to see technology make a tangible difference in society. This chapter of my life reflects a blend of my passion for technology with a commitment to social impact, illustrating how robotics can be a powerful tool for bridging the gap between complex technology and real-world applications.

Discovering the Power of Robotics

My fascination with robotics was sparked by an understanding that robots could do more than just perform tasks; they could transform lives. This realization came from observing everyday technologies and imagining their potential to do extraordinary

things. From automated manufacturing to robotic prosthetics, the versatility and impact of robotics captivated my imagination.

The Inception of the 'Rohbot Kit'

The idea for the 'Rohbot Kit' originated from a simple observation: the disparity in access to educational resources in robotics. I noticed that many students, especially in underprivileged communities, were missing out on learning opportunities in robotics due to lack of resources. Determined to make a difference, I set out to create a robotics kit that was affordable, accessible, and easy to use, even for those with limited access to technology.

Designing and Developing the Kit

The journey from concept to creation was both challenging and rewarding. I started by researching various components, focusing on cost-effectiveness and ease of use. The design phase involved numerous iterations, balancing functionality with simplicity. Building the first prototype was a milestone, bringing my vision one step closer to reality.

Field Testing and Iterations

Testing the 'Rohbot Kit' in real-world scenarios was crucial. I collaborated with local schools and community centers, where I introduced the kit to students. Observing their interactions, gathering feedback, and understanding their needs was instrumental in refining the design. Each iteration brought new improvements, making the kit more user-friendly and effective as a learning tool.

Expanding Reach: Workshops and Demonstrations

To broaden the impact of the project, I organized workshops and demonstrations in various settings, from local communities to international forums. These events were not just about showcasing the kit, but also about igniting a passion for robotics and STEM in young minds. Seeing students' eyes light up as they brought their robots to life was profoundly gratifying.

Learning from the Community

Engaging with the community taught me invaluable lessons. I learned that technology is most powerful when it is inclusive, accessible, and serves a purpose beyond itself. The feedback and experiences of the users were crucial in shaping the evolution of the 'Rohbot Kit.'

Robotics for Social Good

My work with robotics reinforced my belief that technology should be a force for good. I explored how robotics could address broader social issues, from aiding in disaster relief to enhancing education. This exploration was about finding meaningful applications for robotics, where the technology could make a tangible difference in society.

Reflections and Future Aspirations

As I reflect on my journey with robotics, I see it as a convergence of technology, creativity, and social responsibility. It was a journey that went beyond engineering and coding, touching on aspects of design thinking, empathy, and community engagement. Looking ahead, I am excited about the potential of robotics to transform industries and lives, and I remain committed to being a part of this transformative journey.

In this chapter of my life, robotics became more than just a field of study; it became a medium through which I could apply my technical skills to create positive change in the world. It underscored my belief that the true value of technology lies in its ability to improve lives and strengthen societies.

Identifying the Need

The genesis of the Rohbot Kit lay in a simple observation: the vast disparity in access to robotics education. I saw firsthand how students in underprivileged communities were often left behind in the rapidly advancing field of robotics. This realization sparked a desire to create a solution that was not only technologically advanced but also accessible and inclusive.

Conceptualizing the Kit

The initial phase involved conceptualizing what the Rohbot Kit would be. It needed to be affordable, user-friendly, and versatile enough to teach fundamental robotics concepts. The goal was to design a kit that could be used without extensive prior knowledge in robotics or programming, making it suitable for a wide range of learners.

Design Challenges and Breakthroughs

Designing the Rohbot Kit presented numerous challenges. Balancing cost with functionality was a constant struggle. I experimented with various components, from microcontrollers to sensors, to find the perfect blend of affordability and quality. The breakthrough came when I decided to use open-source software and readily available materials, significantly reducing costs without compromising on performance.

Prototyping and Testing

The next step was to build a prototype and test it. This phase was crucial, as it transformed ideas into a tangible product. Testing the prototype in real-world settings, particularly in schools and community centers, provided invaluable feedback. This iterative process of prototyping and testing ensured that the final product was not only functional but also met the needs of its users.

Educational Content and Resources

Developing the educational content and resources that accompanied the kit was as important as the hardware itself. I created a series of tutorials and lesson plans that guided users through the basics of robotics, from assembling the kit to programming it to perform various tasks. This educational material was designed to be engaging and easy to understand, making learning both fun and effective.

Overcoming Obstacles

The journey was fraught with obstacles, from technical setbacks to logistical challenges. There were moments of doubt and frustration, but each obstacle was an opportunity to learn and grow. Perseverance and a problem-solving mindset were key in overcoming these challenges.

The Impact of the Rohbot Kit

The true success of the Rohbot Kit was measured by its impact. Seeing students from diverse backgrounds engage with the kit and develop an interest in robotics was immensely rewarding. The kit not only provided them with technical skills but also inspired creativity and critical thinking.

Reflections on the Journey

Developing the Rohbot Kit was a journey that went beyond engineering and coding. It taught me the importance of empathy in design, the value of perseverance in the face of challenges, and the joy of seeing one's work make a real difference. As I reflect on this journey, I realize that the Rohbot Kit was more than just a product; it was a catalyst for change, a tool for empowerment, and a testament to the power of technology to transform education.

In this chapter, the Rohbot Kit stands as a symbol of my belief that technology should be accessible, educational, and a force for good. It represents a significant stride in my journey, where my passion for technology and commitment to social impact converged to create something meaningful.

Chapter 7: Distributing the Rohbot Kit: Empowering Students in Mexico and Africa

While I personally did not travel to Mexico and Africa, my involvement with the Rohbot Kit transcended physical boundaries. Through a strategic partnership with a company specializing in educational outreach, the Rohbot Kit reached the hands of eager students in these regions, marking a significant milestone in my endeavor to democratize robotics education globally.

Establishing the Partnership

The journey to extend the reach of the Rohbot Kit began with the selection of a suitable partner. I sought a company with a strong presence in international educational projects and a shared vision of making technology accessible. This collaboration was crucial, as it enabled the kit to impact communities far beyond my immediate reach.

Tailoring the Kit for Diverse Audiences

Preparing the Rohbot Kit for students in Mexico and Africa involved more than just shipping boxes. It required careful consideration of the varied educational landscapes, resource availability, and cultural contexts. I worked diligently to ensure the kit was intuitive and user-friendly, with comprehensive instructions that transcended language and cultural barriers.

The Joy of Remote Teaching and Learning

Though I couldn't be there in person, the feedback and images shared by our partner were immensely gratifying. Seeing photographs of children assembling and operating the Rohbot Kit was a surreal experience. Each picture told a story of curiosity, engagement, and joy; it was evident that the kits were more than just educational tools – they were sparks igniting a newfound interest in technology.

Overcoming Challenges through Collaboration

This remote distribution and teaching model presented unique challenges. Ensuring the kits were used effectively required clear communication, well-designed instructional materials, and reliable feedback mechanisms. Collaborating closely with our partner, we tackled these challenges, adapting and refining our approach to enhance the learning experience.

Impact and Reflections

The impact of this initiative went beyond the physical distribution of the kits. It was about inspiring young minds, regardless of their geographical location, and providing them with tools to explore and innovate. The project reinforced my belief in the power of technology as a unifying and empowering force.

Lessons Learned from Remote Outreach

This experience taught me valuable lessons in global outreach, communication, and the importance of adaptability. It showed me that with determination and the right partnerships, it's possible to make a positive impact across the globe, even from afar.

Future Goals for Global Education

Inspired by the success of this project, my future goals include expanding the reach of the Rohbot Kit to more regions around the world. I am committed to refining the kit and its instructional resources to suit a wider array of educational environments and learning styles.

In conclusion, the distribution of the Rohbot Kit to schools in Mexico and Africa represents a significant achievement in my journey. It stands as a testament to the fact that with innovation, collaboration, and a vision, it's possible to bridge educational gaps and inspire the next generation of technologists, regardless of their location or background.

Chapter 8: The Intersection of Neuroscience and Technology

As I ventured deeper into the realms of science and innovation, the intersection of neuroscience and technology emerged as a profound area of exploration. This convergence presented an exciting opportunity to apply technological advancements to understand and enhance brain function, offering groundbreaking approaches to address neurological and cognitive challenges.

In this chapter, my journey takes an intriguing turn into the realm of neuroscience, intertwining my passion for technology with a deep-seated desire to contribute to social good. Here, I explore the intersection of neuroscience with technological innovation, particularly focusing on how this powerful combination can address complex challenges in education and health.

The Allure of Neuroscience

My interest in neuroscience was sparked by a fascination with the human brain, the most complex and enigmatic organ in the body. I was captivated by how neuroscience could unravel mysteries of cognition, learning, and behavior. This curiosity led me to explore how technological advancements could augment our understanding of the brain and address neurological challenges.

Bridging Neuroscience and Technology

The bridge between neuroscience and technology became evident to me through the field of neurotechnology – where brain science converges with engineering. I researched areas like brain-computer interfaces, neuroimaging, and cognitive computing, realizing that technology could be a powerful tool in deciphering and harnessing the brain's capabilities.

The DyslexiaDetect Project

One of the pivotal moments in this chapter was the inception of the DyslexiaDetect project. This endeavor stemmed from a desire to use technology for a meaningful social cause – early and accurate detection of dyslexia. I developed an application using machine learning and eye-tracking technology to identify patterns indicative of dyslexia, aiming to provide an accessible diagnostic tool for schools and parents.

Challenges and Breakthroughs

Developing DyslexiaDetect was replete with challenges. From understanding the complex nature of dyslexia to creating an algorithm that could accurately analyze eye movement data, each phase required patience and innovation. The breakthrough came when I successfully merged the principles of neuroscience with computational techniques, resulting in a tool that could reliably identify dyslexic tendencies.

Community Engagement and Feedback

Testing and refining DyslexiaDetect involved working closely with the community. Collaborating with schools, educators, and healthcare professionals provided valuable insights into the real-world application of the tool. The feedback from these interactions was crucial in fine-tuning the algorithm and making the application more user-friendly.

Impact on Education and Health

The impact of DyslexiaDetect went beyond just technical achievement. It underscored the potential of technology to make a tangible difference in the fields of education and health. The project not only offered an innovative approach to dyslexia detection but also raised awareness about the condition and the importance of early intervention.

Reflections on the Convergence of Disciplines

This venture into neuroscience and social good reinforced my belief in the power of interdisciplinary approaches. It taught me that complex societal challenges often require solutions that transcend traditional boundaries, combining diverse fields like neuroscience, technology, and education.

Looking Ahead: New Frontiers in Neurotechnology

Inspired by the success and impact of DyslexiaDetect, my future aspirations involve exploring new frontiers in neurotechnology. I am particularly interested in how emerging technologies like artificial intelligence and quantum computing can further enhance our understanding and treatment of neurological disorders.

In summary, this chapter of my journey is a testament to the transformative potential of combining neuroscience with technology for social good. It highlights my commitment to using innovative solutions to address educational and health-related challenges, paving the way for a future where technology and neuroscience work hand in hand to improve lives.

Understanding the Brain through Technology

The human brain, a complex and intricate organ, has always been a subject of great intrigue. My journey into neuroscience began with a desire to understand how this organ processes information, learns, and adapts. Technology, especially in the form of neuroimaging tools like fMRI and EEG, provided a window into the brain's workings, allowing scientists to observe neural activity in real time.

Neurotechnology: A New Frontier

Neurotechnology emerged as a field that blended neuroscience with technological innovation, offering new ways to interact with and manipulate the brain. From brain-computer interfaces (BCIs) that translate neural activity into computer commands, to neuroprosthetics that restore lost sensory or motor functions, neurotechnology was redefining the boundaries of what was possible.

The Role of Artificial Intelligence

Artificial intelligence (AI) played a pivotal role in my exploration of neuroscience and technology. AI algorithms, particularly in machine learning and neural networks, mirrored aspects of human cognitive processes, providing insights into learning and decision-making. These technologies not only aided in the analysis of complex neurological data but also offered models to simulate brain functions.

Tackling Neurological Disorders

One of the most compelling aspects of this intersection was its potential to tackle neurological disorders. I was particularly interested in how technology could be used for early detection and intervention in conditions like dyslexia, autism, and Alzheimer's disease. The possibility of developing tools that could change the lives of individuals with these conditions was a driving force behind my research.

Ethical Considerations and Human Impact

Exploring the intersection of neuroscience and technology also brought to light various ethical considerations. Issues such as privacy, consent, and the long-term implications of neurotechnological interventions were critical. It was clear that as we advanced in our capability to interface with the brain, we also needed to be mindful of the ethical and social implications of these technologies.

Collaborations and Interdisciplinary Work

My journey in this field was marked by collaborations with neuroscientists, engineers, and healthcare professionals. This interdisciplinary approach was not only enriching but also essential in addressing the multifaceted challenges at the nexus of neuroscience and technology.

Personal Growth and Future Aspirations

This exploration into the intersection of neuroscience and technology was more than an academic endeavor; it was a journey of personal growth. It challenged me to think critically, approach problems creatively, and consider the broader impact of my work. Looking ahead, I am excited by the prospects of further contributing to this field, driven by the belief that the synergistic power of neuroscience and technology holds the key to many of the challenges we face in healthcare and education.

In conclusion, the intersection of neuroscience and technology is a dynamic and rapidly evolving field, brimming with opportunities for innovation and discovery. My experiences in this area have solidified my commitment to leveraging technology for the betterment of human health and understanding, marking an exciting chapter in my journey of exploration and impact.

Chapter 9: DyslexiaDetect: A Journey of Invention and Empathy

DyslexiaDetect emerged from a confluence of my interest in neuroscience, a deep-seated sense of empathy, and a commitment to leveraging technology for social good. This project was not just a technological venture; it was a personal journey that highlighted the profound impact innovation can have on individual lives and education systems.

The Genesis of DyslexiaDetect

The idea for DyslexiaDetect was born from a simple yet powerful realization: early detection of dyslexia can significantly alter educational outcomes and life trajectories for many children. However, many lack access to early and accurate diagnosis. Motivated by this, I envisioned a tool that could democratize access to dyslexia screening using technology.

Understanding Dyslexia

Before diving into technological solutions, I immersed myself in understanding dyslexia - a learning disorder characterized by difficulties with accurate and/or fluent word recognition and by poor spelling and decoding abilities. This understanding was crucial; it guided the development of DyslexiaDetect to ensure it addressed the specific challenges posed by dyslexia.

Developing the Tool

The development of DyslexiaDetect involved integrating eye-tracking technology with machine learning algorithms. By analyzing patterns in eye movement and fixation, the tool aimed to identify markers indicative of dyslexia. This phase was marked by rigorous testing, algorithm refinement, and continuous learning.

Challenges and Innovations

The journey was filled with challenges. Ensuring accuracy and reliability in the detection process was paramount. I experimented with various machine learning models, continually refining them to improve their predictive capabilities. Innovations were necessary at every turn, from enhancing the eye-tracking algorithm to ensuring the tool's usability for non-technical users.

Collaborations and Feedback

Collaboration was key to the success of DyslexiaDetect. Working with educators, neuroscientists, and psychologists provided valuable insights into the practical application of the tool. Feedback from early users was instrumental in making DyslexiaDetect more user-friendly and effective.

Ethical Considerations and Impact

In developing DyslexiaDetect, I was acutely aware of the ethical implications, especially regarding data privacy and the interpretation of results. It was crucial to handle sensitive information with the utmost care and to provide clear, actionable insights from the screenings.

DyslexiaDetect in Action

Seeing DyslexiaDetect in action was profoundly rewarding. Reports from schools and parents about the tool's effectiveness in identifying dyslexic tendencies among children underscored the impact that thoughtful technological solutions can have in the real world.

Reflecting on the Journey

The journey of creating DyslexiaDetect was as much about technology as it was about empathy and social responsibility. It reinforced my belief in the power of innovation to make a real difference and highlighted the importance of understanding the human element in technological solutions.

Future Aspirations

Inspired by the success of DyslexiaDetect, I am motivated to explore further how technology can be harnessed to address other educational and neurological challenges. This project has opened up new avenues for research and innovation, setting the stage for future endeavors in the intersection of technology, neuroscience, and social impact.

In summary, DyslexiaDetect stands as a testament to the potential of merging technology with empathy to address complex challenges. It encapsulates a journey of invention driven by a desire to create meaningful change, reinforcing my commitment to using my skills and knowledge for the greater good.

Chapter 10: Founding illuminEd Inc.: Vision and Challenges

The founding of illuminEd Inc. marked a pivotal moment in my journey, where my passion for technology and commitment to social impact converged into a singular vision. This endeavor was more than just the creation of a non-profit; it was the embodiment of a dream to use innovation for educational empowerment.

In this chapter, I discuss the entrepreneurial aspects of my journey, highlighting how my passion for technology and social good evolved into innovative ventures. This phase is characterized by the establishment of illuminEd Inc., the launch of various initiatives, and the challenges and triumphs of navigating the entrepreneurial landscape as a young innovator.

The Birth of illuminEd Inc.

The founding of illuminEd Inc. marked a significant milestone in my journey. Driven by a desire to create impactful educational solutions, I, along with a group of like-minded peers, established this non-profit with a mission to democratize access to technology and education for underprivileged communities. This venture was not just about starting a company; it was about creating a platform for change.

Developing a Vision

The vision for illuminEd Inc. was clear from the outset: to leverage technology to bridge educational gaps and empower learners worldwide. This vision guided our projects, from the Rohbot Kit to DyslexiaDetect, and shaped our approach to tackling educational challenges.

Embracing the Entrepreneurial Mindset

Stepping into the role of an entrepreneur required a shift in mindset. It was about being a problem-solver, a risk-taker, and a visionary. I learned to embrace uncertainty, to be resilient in the face of setbacks, and to be adaptable in changing circumstances. These qualities were not just essential for business success; they were life skills that prepared me for future challenges.

Navigating Challenges

The entrepreneurial journey was replete with challenges. From securing funding to managing a team, from legal complexities to market strategies, each hurdle was a learning experience. These challenges taught me the importance of perseverance, strategic thinking, and effective leadership.

Impactful Projects and Initiatives

Under the umbrella of illuminEd Inc., we launched several initiatives that reflected our commitment to social impact. Each project, whether it was a new educational app or a community workshop, was aimed at making a tangible difference in the lives of learners and educators. Seeing our projects come to fruition was a testament to the power of entrepreneurial action in addressing societal issues.

Building a Team and a Community

A crucial aspect of my entrepreneurial journey was building a team that shared our vision and values. Collaborating with a diverse group of individuals, each bringing unique skills and perspectives, was both challenging and enriching. Together, we fostered a community of innovators and educators, united by a common goal.

Learning from Failures and Successes

Entrepreneurship was as much about handling failures as it was about celebrating successes. Each setback was an opportunity to learn and grow. I learned that failure was not the opposite of success but a part of the journey towards it.

The Road Ahead

Looking forward, the entrepreneurial spirit continues to drive me. There are new challenges to face, new problems to solve, and new opportunities to explore. My experiences with illuminEd Inc. have laid a strong foundation for my future endeavors, equipping me with the skills, knowledge, and mindset to continue making a difference.

In summary, this chapter is about the transformation from a technology enthusiast to a social entrepreneur. It highlights my journey of harnessing the power of innovation for social good and underscores the role of entrepreneurial spirit in driving change. Through illuminEd Inc. and its initiatives, I have embarked on a path that not only fosters technological advancement but also contributes to building a more equitable and educated world.

Crafting the Vision

The vision behind illuminEd Inc. was clear and ambitious: to harness cutting-edge technology to bridge educational disparities, particularly in underserved communities. This vision was rooted in my belief that access to quality education and technology should not be a privilege but a right accessible to all. IlluminEd Inc. was conceived as a vehicle to realize this goal, transforming the landscape of educational opportunities through innovative solutions.

The Challenges of Starting a Non-Profit

Embarking on the journey to establish illuminEd Inc. presented a unique set of challenges. The initial phase involved navigating the complexities of legal incorporation, understanding non-profit management, and building a sustainable business model.

Assembling a Team

A critical step in the formation of illuminEd Inc. was assembling a team that shared the vision and possessed the diverse skills necessary to bring our ideas to life. This process involved reaching out to like-minded individuals, from educators to tech enthusiasts, and building a cohesive team united by a common purpose. Balancing team dynamics, fostering collaboration, and leveraging each member's strengths were essential components of our early success.

Developing and Implementing Projects

With a team in place, we focused on developing and implementing projects that aligned with our mission. This included educational programs, technological tools like the Rohbot Kit and DyslexiaDetect, and community workshops. Each project presented its own set of challenges, from design and development to deployment and evaluation. Adapting to these challenges required innovation, flexibility, and a constant focus on our end goals.

Overcoming Operational Hurdles

Operational hurdles were a constant reality. We faced issues ranging from resource limitations to logistical challenges in project implementation. Overcoming these hurdles required strategic planning, efficient resource management, and a willingness to adapt our approaches as needed.

Measuring Impact and Success

Evaluating the impact and success of our initiatives was crucial. We developed metrics and feedback mechanisms to assess our projects' effectiveness and to understand their real-world implications. This continuous process of evaluation and adaptation helped ensure that our efforts were making a tangible difference.

Reflecting on the Journey

Reflecting on the journey of founding and growing illuminEd Inc., I recognize it as a period of immense learning and personal growth. It was a journey that tested my resolve, challenged my capabilities, and reinforced my commitment to using technology for social good. The experience of transforming a vision into a functioning organization has been one of the most challenging yet rewarding aspects of my journey.

Looking Forward

As illuminEd Inc. continues to evolve, the challenges and learning opportunities it presents remain as compelling as ever. The journey ahead is filled with potential for greater impact and innovation. My experience with illuminEd Inc. has not only been a foundational chapter in my entrepreneurial story but also a reaffirmation of my belief in the power of technology to transform education and empower communities.

In conclusion, the founding of illuminEd Inc. is a testament to the power of vision, the importance of perseverance, and the impact of collaborative effort. It stands as a beacon of my entrepreneurial spirit and my commitment to making a positive difference in the world through education and technology.

Chapter 11: The Kickstarter Campaign: Lessons in Crowdfunding

Launching a Kickstarter campaign for the Rohbot Kit was a significant step in the journey of illuminEd Inc. This endeavor was not just about raising funds; it was an exercise in community engagement, marketing, and learning the intricacies of crowdfunding. The campaign provided invaluable lessons in entrepreneurship and the power of collective support.

Preparing for the Campaign

Preparation was key to our Kickstarter campaign. This stage involved defining our goals, creating a compelling narrative around the Rohbot Kit, and producing engaging multimedia content to showcase our project. We also had to set realistic funding targets and develop attractive rewards for backers. This preparatory phase taught us the importance of a clear and compelling pitch in crowdfunding.

Launching the Campaign

The launch of the campaign was both exciting and nerve-wracking. We announced it through various channels, including social media, email newsletters, and community forums. The initial response was crucial, and we worked tirelessly to spread the word and generate excitement around our project.

Engaging with the Community

One of the most crucial aspects of our Kickstarter campaign was community engagement. We interacted with backers, answered queries, and provided regular updates. This engagement was not just about keeping backers informed; it was about building a community of supporters who were invested in our vision and success.

Overcoming Challenges

The campaign had its share of challenges. One significant hurdle was maintaining momentum after the initial surge of support. We learned that continuous engagement and promotion were essential to keep the campaign in the public eye. Additionally, addressing backers' concerns and being transparent about our progress and challenges helped maintain trust and support.

Navigating the Complexities of Crowdfunding

Crowdfunding was more complex than we initially anticipated. We had to manage logistics like reward fulfillment, track funding progress, and adhere to Kickstarter's policies and timelines. These responsibilities taught us valuable lessons in project management and accountability.

Reflecting on Success and Learning

Upon successfully meeting our funding goal, we took time to reflect on the lessons learned. The success of the campaign was a validation of our idea and a testament to the power of community support. We also acknowledged areas for improvement, such as scaling our outreach efforts and streamlining our communication strategies.

The Impact of the Campaign

The Kickstarter campaign had a significant impact beyond just financial backing. It raised awareness about our project and mission, attracting interest from educators, tech enthusiasts, and potential collaborators. The campaign also served as a launchpad for further development and distribution of the Rohbot Kit.

Moving Forward

The experience of running a Kickstarter campaign provided a foundation for future crowdfunding endeavors. It instilled confidence in our team and reinforced our commitment to the vision of illuminEd Inc. As we move forward, the lessons learned from this campaign will inform our strategies in marketing, community engagement, and project management.

In summary, the Kickstarter campaign for the Rohbot Kit was a crucial learning experience in crowdfunding and community building. It underscored the challenges and rewards of bringing an innovative idea to a broad audience and solidified our capabilities as young entrepreneurs in the field of educational technology.

Chapter 12: Experiences at PRISMS: Leading and Learning

My time at PRISMS (Princeton International School of Mathematics and Science) was a transformative period that blended leadership and learning in a unique and enriching way. At PRISMS, I not only advanced my academic pursuits but also honed my leadership skills, particularly through my involvement in the robotics team and various STEM initiatives.

Thriving in an Academically Rigorous Environment

PRISMS provided an academically rigorous environment that pushed me to excel in my studies. The school's focus on mathematics, science, and technology resonated deeply with my interests, and I embraced the challenging curriculum with enthusiasm. This setting allowed me to explore complex subjects in depth and fostered a culture of intellectual curiosity.

This chapter of my journey underscores my experiences as a leader within the academic world, where I balanced the rigors of advanced learning with the responsibilities of guiding and inspiring others. My tenure as the captain of the robotics team, in particular, stands out as a defining aspect of my leadership role.

Embracing Academic Challenges

Throughout my academic career, I eagerly embraced complex subjects, from quantum computing to neuroscience. This pursuit was not merely about learning; it was about cultivating a mindset of curiosity, problem-solving, and resilience, essential qualities for any leader.

Leading the Robotics Team

As the captain of the robotics team, I had the unique opportunity to merge my passion for technology with leadership. This role involved strategizing, team coordination, and mentoring peers in robotics design and competition. Leading the team was a profound exercise in teamwork, communication, and the practical application of technical skills.

Academic Leadership and Collaboration

In various academic clubs and societies, I played a pivotal role, driving initiatives that promoted a culture of innovation and collaborative learning. From organizing STEM events to leading academic projects, I focused on creating environments that encouraged creativity and collective problem-solving.

Mentoring and Educational Outreach

Mentoring younger students and peers, especially in robotics and STEM subjects, was a cornerstone of my leadership experience. This role honed my ability to communicate complex concepts clearly and reinforced the importance of empathy and adaptability in teaching.

Spearheading Research and Innovation

My leadership extended to initiating academic research projects, often collaborating with educators and industry experts. These ventures allowed me to apply theoretical knowledge in practical settings, further deepening my understanding and skills in various subjects.

Overcoming Leadership Challenges

Navigating the dual responsibilities of academic excellence and team leadership presented its own set of challenges. I learned valuable lessons in time management, prioritization, and the nuances of leading diverse teams towards common objectives.

Enriching the School Community

My goal was always to enrich the school's academic and extracurricular landscape. I strived to create an inclusive environment that valued intellectual curiosity and celebrated collaborative achievement, leaving a positive imprint on the school community.

Reflecting on Leadership Growth

Reflecting on my experiences, I recognize the profound impact that academic leadership has had on my personal and professional development. It has ingrained in me the values of resilience, teamwork, and the transformative power of leading by example.

Future Aspirations in Leadership

Looking forward, I view my experiences in academic leadership, particularly as the robotics captain, as foundational to my future endeavors. Whether in college or beyond, these experiences have equipped me with the skills and perspective to continue making impactful contributions in any collaborative setting.

In summary, this chapter encapsulates my journey of academic leadership, highlighted by my role as the robotics team captain. It illustrates how leadership in academia is not just about personal achievement but about inspiring, guiding, and collaborating with others to foster a culture of innovation and collective success.

Leading the Robotics Team

As the captain of the robotics team at PRISMS, I had the opportunity to lead a group of talented and like-minded peers. This role involved strategizing for competitions, managing team dynamics, and mentoring team members in both technical and soft skills. My leadership in this area was not just about achieving competitive success; it was about fostering a collaborative and innovative spirit within the team.

Mentorship and Peer Learning

At PRISMS, I actively engaged in mentorship roles, helping my peers in subjects where I had expertise. This experience was mutually beneficial – it reinforced my own understanding and honed my skills in communicating complex ideas effectively. Peer learning sessions became a cornerstone of my academic experience, highlighting the importance of collaborative learning.

Engaging in Research and Projects

PRISMS provided ample opportunities for engaging in research and innovative projects. I took advantage of these opportunities to explore topics that intersected with my interests in technology and neuroscience. These projects allowed me to apply theoretical knowledge in practical scenarios, enhancing my understanding and skills.

Navigating Academic and Leadership Roles

Balancing my academic responsibilities with leadership roles was a significant learning experience. It taught me valuable lessons in time management, prioritization, and resilience. These skills proved invaluable in handling the rigorous demands of both academics and extracurricular activities.

Contributing to the School Community

My aim at PRISMS was to contribute positively to the school community. I participated in and organized events that promoted STEM education, shared my knowledge and experience with younger students, and endeavored to leave a lasting impact on the school's culture of innovation and collaboration.

Reflecting on Personal Growth

Reflecting on my time at PRISMS, I see a period of significant personal and professional growth. The experiences I had – from leading the robotics team to engaging in challenging academic work – shaped my understanding of effective leadership and the value of a collaborative approach to education.

Looking Ahead

As I look towards the future, the lessons learned and experiences gained at PRISMS will undoubtedly influence my approach to both academic and professional challenges. The blend of leadership and learning that I experienced at PRISMS has equipped me with a solid foundation to excel in future endeavors.

In conclusion, my experiences at PRISMS represent a critical phase of my journey, where the dual paths of academic excellence and leadership converged. This period was instrumental in shaping me into a well-rounded individual, ready to face the challenges of higher education and beyond with confidence and a spirit of innovation.

Chapter 13: Advanced Studies at Princeton and Online Macroeconomics Course at JHU

My academic journey was significantly enriched by advanced studies in mathematics at Princeton University and complemented by an online course in Macroeconomics through Johns Hopkins University (JHU). This blend of deep mathematical theory and economic understanding presented a holistic and interdisciplinary approach to my education.

Deepening Mathematical Understanding at Princeton

At Princeton, my engagement with challenging mathematical concepts, particularly in Number Theory and Real Analysis, pushed my cognitive boundaries. These courses were not just about learning complex mathematical theories; they were an exercise in critical thinking, problem-solving, and logical reasoning, preparing me for a wide range of intellectual challenges.

Exploring Macroeconomics at JHU

Simultaneously, I pursued an interest in economics through an online Macroeconomics course offered by JHU. This course allowed me to explore economic theories and principles, understanding the broader economic forces that shape global markets and societies. The online format provided flexibility and accessibility, enabling me to balance it with my rigorous studies at Princeton.

Integrating Mathematics and Economics

The combination of advanced mathematics and macroeconomics created a unique educational experience. It allowed me to see the interplay between abstract mathematical theories and practical economic models, enhancing my analytical skills and understanding of real-world economic issues.

The Online Learning Experience

The online Macroeconomics course at JHU was an exercise in self-discipline and independent learning. It required effective time management and self-motivation, skills that are essential in today's increasingly digital and self-directed learning environments.

Broadening Perspectives

Studying macroeconomics expanded my perspective beyond the technical and theoretical realms of mathematics. It equipped me with a broader understanding of global economic systems, an appreciation for economic policy, and insights into how economic theories can be applied to address societal challenges.

Navigating Hybrid Learning Environments

Balancing in-person courses at Princeton with an online course at JHU highlighted the importance of adaptability in modern education. This hybrid learning approach underscored the evolving nature of academic pursuit in a world where traditional and digital learning environments coexist.

Reflecting on Academic Growth

Reflecting on my time at Princeton and JHU, I recognize the immense value these experiences added to my academic portfolio. They provided a well-rounded educational experience, fostering both deep specialization and broad understanding.

Future Academic and Professional Aspirations

As I move forward, the skills and knowledge gained from these diverse academic experiences form a strong foundation for my future endeavors. The combination of advanced mathematics and macroeconomics has prepared me to approach problems with a comprehensive, interdisciplinary perspective, which is crucial in an increasingly complex and interconnected world.

In conclusion, my advanced studies at Princeton, combined with the online macroeconomics course at JHU, have been integral to my academic development. They have not only enriched my knowledge base but also enhanced my ability to analyze, integrate, and apply diverse concepts across disciplines. This educational journey has been a testament to the value of a multifaceted and integrative approach to learning

Chapter 14: Volunteering with FEMA: Leadership in Crisis

My experience volunteering with the Federal Emergency Management Agency (FEMA) stands out as a pivotal chapter in my journey, underscoring the critical role of leadership in times of crisis. This period was not only about contributing to disaster management efforts but also about gaining invaluable insights into the dynamics of leadership under challenging circumstances.

In this chapter, I recount my experiences with community engagement and service, which form a crucial part of my journey. These experiences have not only allowed me to contribute positively to society but also provided invaluable lessons in empathy, leadership, and the impact of proactive civic involvement.

Volunteering with FEMA

One of the most formative aspects of my community service was volunteering with the Federal Emergency Management Agency (FEMA). This involvement gave me firsthand experience in disaster response and emergency management. It taught me the significance of preparedness, quick decision-making, and the intricate coordination required in managing large-scale emergencies.

Engaging with Local Schools and Educational Initiatives

My commitment to community service extended to local schools and educational programs. I took an active role in organizing workshops, tutoring sessions, and STEM activities. These interactions were not just about teaching or imparting knowledge; they were opportunities to inspire and ignite a passion for learning in others.

The Power of Technology in Community Service

Through my involvement in various projects, like the development and distribution of the Rohbot Kit, I experienced how technology could be a powerful tool for community service. It allowed me to reach out to underserved communities, providing educational resources and sparking interest in STEM fields among young learners.

Collaborating with Non-Profit Organizations

Collaboration with non-profit organizations broadened the scope of my community engagement. Working with these organizations, I learned how to effectively channel my efforts and resources to address specific community needs. These collaborations also offered insights into the challenges and complexities of social work.

Leadership Roles in Community Projects

Taking on leadership roles in community projects was a significant aspect of my service. Whether it was organizing a fundraiser or leading a team in a community development project, each role helped me develop my leadership skills. These experiences taught me how to motivate teams, manage resources, and drive projects towards successful outcomes.

Learning from the Community

Interacting with diverse groups within the community was an education in itself. It provided me with a deeper understanding of societal issues and the varied challenges faced by different groups. These interactions were humbling and enriching, and they played a key role in shaping my perspectives on social responsibility.

Reflecting on the Impact of Service

Reflecting on my community engagement and service, I realize the profound impact these experiences have had on my personal and professional growth. They have instilled in me a sense of responsibility towards society and reinforced the belief that individual efforts can lead to significant positive change.

Future Commitments to Community Service

Looking ahead, I remain committed to community service and engagement. I plan to continue leveraging my skills and knowledge to contribute to societal well-being and to encourage others to do the same. These experiences have cemented my belief in the power of collective effort in making a difference in the world.

In summary, Chapter 7 highlights the importance of community engagement and service in my journey. It underscores how active involvement in community initiatives not only benefits society but also contributes to personal development, fostering a sense of empathy, leadership, and civic responsibility. These experiences have been fundamental in shaping my character and will continue to influence my future endeavors in positive and impactful ways.

Understanding the Scope of Emergency Management

Volunteering with FEMA exposed me to the complexities of emergency management. I learned about the intricacies of planning, coordination, and execution required in responding to large-scale disasters like hurricanes, floods, and other catastrophic events. This exposure provided a real-world context to the theoretical knowledge I had gained about crisis management.

Training and Preparation

As a volunteer, I underwent extensive training to equip myself with the skills necessary for effective disaster response. This training included understanding FEMA's emergency response protocols, rapid needs assessment, and the Incident Command System. These preparatory courses were critical in helping me understand how to operate effectively in high-pressure situations.

On-the-Ground Experience

The on-the-ground experience with FEMA was both challenging and enlightening. I had the opportunity to be part of response teams that worked directly in affected areas. These experiences taught me about the importance of quick decision-making, adaptability, and maintaining a calm demeanor in the face of adversity.

Leadership in Crisis Situations

One of the key lessons from my time with FEMA was understanding the nuances of leadership in crisis situations. Leading or participating in response efforts during emergencies required a balance of assertiveness and empathy, clear communication, and the ability to make swift decisions. It was a testament to the fact that effective leadership can significantly influence the outcome in critical situations.

Collaborative Efforts and Teamwork

Working with FEMA highlighted the importance of teamwork and collaboration. In crisis situations, harmonious coordination among various agencies, volunteers, and local communities is crucial. I learned how to work effectively in teams, contributing my skills while also learning from the experiences and expertise of others.

Gaining a Broader Perspective on Service

Volunteering with FEMA broadened my perspective on service and community engagement. It reinforced the idea that serving the community, especially in times of need, is a profound way to make a tangible difference in people's lives.

Reflecting on Personal Growth and Future Aspirations

Reflecting on my experiences with FEMA, I realize how these have contributed significantly to my personal growth, particularly in developing leadership skills suited to high-stakes environments. As I look to the future, I am inspired to continue developing these skills and applying them in various aspects of my life and career.

Continuing the Commitment to Serve

My commitment to service, particularly in emergency management, remains strong. I plan to continue my involvement with FEMA or similar organizations, leveraging my experiences to contribute effectively to disaster response and preparedness initiatives.

In conclusion, volunteering with FEMA was an integral part of my journey, providing a unique perspective on leadership, teamwork, and service. It was an experience that not only contributed to my personal development but also solidified my commitment to serving the community in times of crisis.

Chapter 15: Initiatives for Social Equity and Inclusion

My commitment to social equity and inclusion has been a driving force behind many of my endeavors. Recognizing the disparities and challenges in various communities, I have been actively involved in initiatives aimed at promoting equality, access, and opportunities for all. These efforts reflect my belief that meaningful change comes from intentional actions geared towards building a more inclusive society.

Understanding the Need for Equity and Inclusion

My journey into social equity began with an awareness of the disparities that exist in education, technology access, and socio-economic opportunities. This awareness was a call to action, prompting me to think critically about how I could contribute to addressing these inequalities.

Developing Inclusive Educational Tools

A significant part of my work in promoting social equity has been through the development and distribution of inclusive educational tools, like the Rohbot Kit. This initiative was specifically designed to make learning in STEM accessible to underprivileged and marginalized communities. By providing these tools, I aimed to bridge the gap in educational resources and empower students from diverse backgrounds.

Collaborating with Non-profits and Community Organizations

Collaboration with non-profit organizations and community groups has been key to my efforts in promoting social equity. Working with these organizations provided insights into the specific needs of different communities and allowed me to tailor my initiatives to have the most significant impact.

Advocacy and Awareness Campaigns

Part of my commitment to social equity involved advocacy and raising awareness about the importance of inclusion and diversity. This included organizing and participating in workshops, seminars, and discussions that highlighted issues of disparity and the importance of inclusive practices in education and technology.

Mentorship Programs for Underserved Youth

I have been involved in mentorship programs targeting underserved youth. These programs focused on providing guidance, support, and resources to help these young individuals in their academic and personal development. By sharing knowledge and experiences, I aimed to inspire and empower them to pursue their goals and aspirations.

Reflecting on the Challenges and Rewards

While working on these initiatives, I encountered various challenges, including resource limitations and differing needs across communities. These challenges, however, were outweighed by the rewards of seeing the positive impact of these efforts. Witnessing the growth, enthusiasm, and potential of the individuals and communities I worked with has been incredibly fulfilling.

Personal Growth and Future Goals

These initiatives for social equity and inclusion have contributed significantly to my personal growth. They have enhanced my understanding of societal issues, honed my leadership skills, and reinforced my commitment to social responsibility. Going forward, I aim to continue these efforts, exploring new ways to promote equity and inclusion in every community I engage with.

In conclusion, my initiatives for social equity and inclusion are an integral part of my journey. They underscore my commitment to creating a more equitable and inclusive world. These experiences have not only shaped my perspective on social issues but have also empowered me to continue working towards a future where opportunities and resources are accessible to everyone, regardless of their background.

Chapter 16: Juggling Academics, Hobbies, and Personal Growth

In this section of my journey, I go deeper into the intricate process of juggling academic responsibilities, personal hobbies, and overall personal growth. This juggling act is a crucial aspect of my story, illustrating how diverse experiences and interests contribute to a well-rounded and fulfilling life.

In this chapter, I reflect on the delicate yet crucial art of balancing diverse aspects of my life - academics, leadership, community service, and personal interests. This balancing act has been a cornerstone of my journey, teaching me invaluable lessons in time management, prioritization, and the importance of well-roundedness.

Juggling Academic Rigor and Extracurricular Leadership

My academic pursuits at institutions like Princeton and participation in advanced online courses demanded a high level of intellectual engagement and time commitment. Simultaneously, leading initiatives like the robotics team and managing projects under illuminEd Inc. required a different set of leadership and organizational skills. Striking a balance between these demanding roles taught me to prioritize effectively and allocate my time in a way that maximized productivity and impact.

Engaging in Community Service

My commitment to community service, especially through FEMA and local educational initiatives, often coincided with my academic and leadership responsibilities. I learned to integrate these service activities into my routine, viewing them not as additional tasks but as integral parts of my personal and professional growth.

Pursuing Personal Interests and Well-being

Amidst these commitments, I also recognized the importance of pursuing personal interests and ensuring well-being. Engaging in hobbies, spending time with family and friends, and practicing self-care were essential to maintaining a healthy balance. These activities provided a necessary respite from my academic and professional endeavors, recharging me and enhancing my overall effectiveness.

Learning from Overcommitment

There were moments when the challenge of balancing numerous responsibilities led to feelings of being overcommitted. These instances were crucial learning opportunities. They taught me the limits of my capacity and the importance of saying no when necessary. From these experiences, I learned to be more mindful of my commitments and to focus on quality rather than quantity.

The Role of Support Systems

The support from mentors, peers, family, and friends was invaluable in maintaining this balance. Their guidance, understanding, and assistance played a significant role in helping me manage my various responsibilities. I learned that seeking help and relying on a support system is not a sign of weakness but a smart strategy for achieving balance.

Adapting to Changing Circumstances

My journey also taught me the importance of adaptability. Circumstances change, and with them, priorities and responsibilities also shift. Being flexible and open to change was crucial in maintaining a healthy balance across different areas of my life.

Reflections on the Importance of Balance

Reflecting on the art of balance, I realize its importance in personal and professional development. Balancing diverse aspects of life has not only made me more resilient and versatile but has also enriched my experiences, providing a more holistic perspective on life and work.

The Academic Endeavor

My academic journey has always been at the forefront, marked by rigorous coursework and in-depth research. Balancing advanced studies in mathematics at Princeton with the online Macroeconomics course at JHU presented a challenging yet rewarding endeavor. These academic pursuits required dedicated focus, discipline, and a deep commitment to learning.

Embracing Hobbies and Interests

Amidst the academic rigor, I actively engaged in hobbies and personal interests. These activities, were not mere pastimes; they were essential for my mental and emotional well-being. They provided a necessary counterbalance to academic pressures, allowing me to unwind and engage in creative and recreational pursuits.

Personal Growth Outside Academia

Personal growth for me extended beyond the confines of academic achievements. It involved developing soft skills, such as communication, empathy, and leadership, often through my roles in various extracurricular activities and community service. These experiences were crucial in building a strong character and honing life skills that are essential in both personal and professional spheres.

Learning Time Management and Prioritization

One of the key lessons in juggling academics, hobbies, and personal growth was mastering the art of time management and prioritization. I learned to allocate my time effectively, ensuring that

I could excel in my studies while also dedicating time to hobbies and personal development activities. This skill has been vital in maintaining a healthy balance and avoiding burnout.

The Role of Reflection and Mindfulness

Regular reflection and mindfulness practices played a significant role in managing this balance. Taking time to reflect on my goals, progress, and well-being helped me stay aligned with my values and aspirations. Mindfulness practices, such as meditation, provided a sense of calm and clarity, especially during periods of high stress.

The Impact of a Supportive Environment

The support from family, friends, and mentors was instrumental in this balancing act. Their encouragement and understanding provided the motivation and strength needed to pursue my diverse interests. This supportive environment was a cornerstone of my ability to manage various aspects of my life effectively.

Continuous Learning and Adaptation

My journey taught me that balance is not a static state but a continuous process of learning and adaptation. As my interests and responsibilities evolved, so did my approach to balancing them. I learned to be flexible, to reassess my priorities, and to make adjustments as needed.

Future Aspirations in Maintaining Balance

Looking ahead, I am committed to maintaining this balance as I embark on new challenges and opportunities. The lessons learned in juggling academics, hobbies, and personal growth will continue to guide me, ensuring that I lead a well-rounded, productive, and satisfying life.

In conclusion, the ability to juggle academics, hobbies, and personal growth has been a defining aspect of my journey. It has taught me the importance of a holistic approach to life, where intellectual pursuits, personal interests, and overall well-being are all given their due importance. This balance has been crucial in shaping me into a versatile, resilient, and well-rounded individual, prepared to navigate the complexities of life with confidence and purpose.

Future Aspirations and Continued Growth

As I look to the future, I carry with me the lessons learned from balancing various aspects of my life. These experiences will continue to guide me in my academic, professional, and personal endeavors, ensuring that I lead a balanced and fulfilling life.

In summary, this chapter encapsulates the essence of balance in my journey. It highlights how managing different facets of life is an art that requires constant learning and adaptation. The experiences and lessons from this balancing act have been fundamental in shaping a well-rounded and grounded individual, ready to face the complexities of life with confidence and poise.

Chapter 17: Embracing Science Fiction and Creative Pursuits

In this segment of my journey, I share the significance of embracing science fiction and other creative pursuits. This aspect of my life highlights the value of imagination, creativity, and the influence of diverse interests in shaping a well-rounded personality.

Science Fiction: A Gateway to Imagination

My fascination with science fiction has been more than just a hobby; it's been a gateway to boundless imagination and inspiration. Engaging with science fiction through literature, movies, and art has allowed me to explore futuristic concepts and innovative ideas, fueling my passion for science and technology. It has provided a creative outlet and a means to visualize the possibilities of future technological advancements.

Creative Expression through Art and Writing

Alongside my interest in science fiction, I have pursued creative expression through art and writing. These activities have been vital for personal expression and mental relaxation. They have allowed me to communicate ideas and emotions in ways that academic pursuits alone could not, fostering a balance between analytical thinking and creative exploration.

Impact on Academic and Professional Interests

My engagement with science fiction and creative arts has significantly impacted my academic and professional interests. It has inspired innovative approaches in my projects and research, encouraging me to think outside the box and approach problems with a creative mindset. This blend of creativity and technical acumen has been instrumental in developing unique solutions to complex challenges.

Building a Diverse Skill Set

Through these creative pursuits, I have developed a diverse skill set. Skills such as critical thinking, storytelling, and visual communication have enhanced my abilities in various domains, from academic research to leadership roles. They have also contributed to my personal development, making me a more empathetic and well-rounded individual.

Community Engagement and Sharing Passions

Embracing science fiction and creative pursuits has also opened opportunities for community engagement. Whether it's participating in science fiction forums, art exhibitions, or writing blogs, these platforms have allowed me to connect with like-minded individuals and share my passions, fostering a sense of community and shared interest.

Overcoming Stereotypes and Encouraging Diversity

My involvement in these fields has also been about breaking stereotypes, especially in the tech and science domains, where creative pursuits are often undervalued. I have advocated for the importance of creativity in scientific fields, encouraging others to embrace diverse interests and perspectives.

Reflecting on the Role of Creativity in Life

Reflecting on my engagement with science fiction and creative arts, I recognize the profound impact they have had on my life. They have not only provided a source of joy and relaxation but have also enriched my professional endeavors and contributed to a more holistic view of the world.

Future Aspirations in Creative Endeavors

Looking forward, I plan to continue integrating my love for science fiction and creative expression into my future projects and career. I believe that this integration will not only enhance my personal fulfillment but also inspire innovative thinking in whatever path I choose to pursue.

In conclusion, embracing science fiction and creative pursuits has been an essential part of my journey, providing a balance to my academic and technical endeavors. It has taught me the value of imagination, creativity, and the importance of nurturing diverse interests to build a multifaceted and enriching life experience.

Chapter 18: The Future of Quantum Computing and AI

In this section, I dive into my perspectives on the future convergence of quantum computing and artificial intelligence (AI), two fields that have profoundly shaped my academic and research interests. This contemplation is rooted in both my fascination with their current capabilities and my anticipation of their potential future impact.

Quantum Computing: Beyond Classical Limits

Quantum computing, with its ability to perform complex calculations at unprecedented speeds, promises to transcend the limitations of classical computing. I predict that in the future, quantum computing will achieve major breakthroughs in areas that are currently computationally infeasible. This includes solving complex optimization problems, revolutionizing cryptography with quantum-resistant algorithms, and enabling new discoveries in physics and chemistry through advanced simulations.

Synergy of Quantum Computing and AI

The intersection of quantum computing and AI presents a particularly intriguing future. Quantum algorithms have the potential to drastically enhance AI's learning and processing capabilities. I envision quantum AI algorithms that can analyze vast datasets more efficiently, leading to breakthroughs in machine learning, pattern recognition, and predictive modeling.

Advancements in Quantum Machine Learning

Quantum machine learning, a nascent field, is likely to see significant growth. This field combines quantum computing's power with AI's adaptability, potentially leading to more sophisticated and efficient learning models. Quantum neural networks and quantum-enhanced optimization are areas that I believe will see substantial advancements, offering new ways to tackle complex, multidimensional problems.

AI's Role in Advancing Quantum Computing

Conversely, AI will play a critical role in advancing quantum computing. AI algorithms can be used to optimize quantum circuit designs, error correction, and system diagnostics. This symbiotic relationship between AI and quantum computing is likely to accelerate the progress in both fields.

Ethical Implications and Societal Impact

With these advancements, however, come significant ethical implications and societal impacts. The integration of quantum computing in AI raises questions about data privacy, security, and the potential for misuse. It's crucial to establish ethical guidelines and robust security protocols to govern the use of these powerful technologies.

Preparing for a Quantum-AI Future

As we move towards this quantum-AI future, it is imperative to prepare the current and next generations of scientists, engineers, and policymakers. Education systems will need to adapt to provide the necessary skills and knowledge, emphasizing not only technical proficiency but also ethical and critical thinking.My Role in Shaping the Future

In this evolving landscape, I see myself contributing to the development and responsible implementation of quantum AI technologies. Whether it's through research, innovation, or advocacy, I am committed to being part of the dialogue and development that will shape this exciting and challenging future.

In conclusion, the future of quantum computing and AI is poised to be a pivotal chapter in our technological evolution. While it promises unprecedented advancements and capabilities, it also demands careful consideration of its ethical and societal implications. As someone deeply invested in these fields, I look forward to contributing to their responsible growth and exploring their potential to transform our world.

In this chapter, I explore my visions and predictions for the future of technology, drawing upon my experiences and learnings. This speculative exploration reflects my deep-seated interest in how technological advancements could shape our future world, both solving current challenges and presenting new ones.

Anticipating the Evolution of AI and Machine Learning

Given my background and interest in AI and machine learning, I foresee significant advancements in these areas. I predict that AI will become more integrated into daily life, enhancing everything from personalized healthcare to streamlined urban planning. Machine learning algorithms will likely become more efficient and capable, potentially achieving breakthroughs in understanding complex systems like climate change and human cognition.

The Future of Quantum Computing

My engagement with quantum computing leads me to envision a future where quantum technologies revolutionize fields such as cryptography, material science, and drug discovery. I predict that quantum computers will solve problems currently intractable for classical computers, leading to significant scientific advancements.

Robotics and Automation

In the realm of robotics, I anticipate advancements that will make robots more autonomous, adaptive, and sensitive to human needs. The integration of robotics in everyday life could range from domestic assistance to more complex roles in industries such as logistics, manufacturing, and healthcare. However, this will also bring challenges in terms of workforce adaptation and ethical considerations. Sustainable Technology and Environmental Solutions

Given the escalating concerns about climate change and environmental sustainability, I foresee a surge in green technologies. Innovations in renewable energy, sustainable manufacturing processes, and waste management are likely to become critical areas of focus. I believe technology will play a key role in combating environmental challenges and promoting sustainable practices.

The Intersection of Neuroscience and Technology

The convergence of neuroscience and technology, particularly in periprosthetic and brain-computer interfaces, is another area I expect to see significant growth. These advancements could lead to enhanced rehabilitation techniques for neurological disorders and new ways of interacting with technology, blurring the lines between human cognition and artificial intelligence.

Challenges and Ethical Considerations

With these technological advancements, I also predict that we will face new ethical dilemmas and societal challenges. Issues around data privacy, AI ethics, and the societal impact of automation will require careful consideration and proactive policy-making to ensure that technological progress benefits society as a whole.

Continuous Learning and Adaptation

As I look to the future, I am committed to staying informed and adaptable in the face of rapid technological changes. Keeping abreast of emerging technologies and their implications will be crucial in navigating the future landscape effectively.

Inspiring and Preparing the Next Generation

Finally, I see myself playing a role in preparing the next generation for this future. Through education, mentorship, and advocacy, I aim to inspire young minds to engage with technology thoughtfully and creatively, equipping them with the skills and perspectives necessary to thrive in a tech-driven future.

In conclusion, this chapter encapsulates my visions and predictions for the future of technology. It reflects a blend of optimism and caution, acknowledging the potential of technological advancements to transform our world for the better while also recognizing the challenges and responsibilities that come with such progress. My journey thus far has prepared me to not only witness but also contribute to this exciting and dynamic future.

Chapter 19: Robotics and Social Impact: What Lies Ahead

In this section, I explore the future intersection of robotics with social impact, focusing on how advancements in robotics could reshape various aspects of society. My experiences and insights lead me to anticipate a future where robotics not only transforms technology but also significantly contributes to solving societal challenges.

Advancements in Human-Centric Robotics

I foresee a future where advancements in robotics will increasingly focus on human-centric applications. This includes the development of robots that can assist in healthcare, such as performing delicate surgeries or providing care for the elderly and disabled. Human-centric robotics will prioritize empathy and understanding, enhancing the quality of life and augmenting human capabilities.

Robotics in Education and Accessibility

In the realm of education, robotics is poised to play a transformative role. Educational robots can provide personalized learning experiences, making education more accessible and inclusive. I envision robots not only as tools for teaching STEM subjects but also as aids that can help bridge learning gaps, especially for students with special educational needs.

Environmental and Disaster Response Robotics

The application of robotics in environmental conservation and disaster response is another area with significant potential for social impact. Robots equipped to handle hazardous environments can be crucial in disaster relief operations, wildlife conservation, and tackling environmental crises like pollution and climate change.

Ethical Manufacturing and Labor Considerations

As robotics becomes more integrated into manufacturing and labor, ethical considerations will become increasingly important. The shift towards automation must be balanced with the impact on the workforce. I believe the future will involve creating strategies that integrate robotic automation in a way that complements human labor rather than replacing it, focusing on upskilling and reskilling workers.

Addressing Social and Economic Disparities

Robotics has the potential to address social and economic disparities. By automating tasks in underserved communities, robotics can enhance productivity and provide new opportunities. However, it's crucial to ensure that the benefits of robotic technology are accessible to all sectors of society, avoiding widening the existing digital divide.

Collaborative Robotics (Cobots)

The development of collaborative robots, or cobots, which work alongside humans, will likely be a significant trend. These cobots can enhance workplace efficiency and safety, especially in industries like manufacturing, logistics, and healthcare.

My Role in Shaping the Future of Robotics

Looking ahead, I see my role in this future as both a contributor and an advocate. I aim to be involved in developing robotics technologies that prioritize social good and to advocate for policies and practices that ensure equitable and ethical use of robotics.

Preparing for a Robotic-Integrated Society

As we progress towards a more robotic-integrated society, it is imperative to prepare communities for this transition. This preparation involves not only technical training but also fostering an understanding of how robotics can be used responsibly to enhance societal well-being.

In conclusion, the future of robotics and its impact on society is a multifaceted area with immense potential. While the technological advancements in robotics promise to bring about significant changes, it is equally important to address the societal, ethical, and economic implications of these changes. My vision for the future is one where robotics is leveraged not just for technological advancement, but as a tool for positive social impact and a catalyst for a more equitable and sustainable world.

Chapter 20: Core Principles of Teen Leadership

As a guide for aspiring young leaders, I've distilled my experiences and observations into core principles that are particularly relevant for teenagers stepping into leadership roles. These principles are designed to navigate the unique challenges and opportunities that come with being a young leader.

In this final chapter, I share the leadership lessons I've learned throughout my journey, aimed at guiding and inspiring young innovators. These lessons, drawn from my experiences in academia, community service, and technology innovation, are intended to provide a roadmap for those embarking on their own paths of discovery and leadership.

Embrace Curiosity and Continuous Learning

My first lesson is the importance of maintaining an insatiable curiosity and a commitment to lifelong learning. The world of technology and innovation is ever-evolving, and staying informed and adaptable is crucial. Young innovators should embrace new challenges, continuously seek knowledge, and remain open to learning from both successes and failures.

Cultivate a Problem-Solving Mindset

Leadership in innovation requires a problem-solving mindset. This involves thinking critically, approaching problems with creativity, and being willing to explore unconventional solutions. Young leaders should be encouraged to view challenges as opportunities to innovate and make a difference.

Foster Collaboration and Teamwork

Innovation rarely happens in isolation. It's vital to understand the power of collaboration and teamwork. Young innovators should learn to work effectively with diverse teams, valuing different perspectives and leveraging collective strengths to achieve common goals.

Balance Confidence with Humility

While confidence is key in leadership, it's equally important to pair it with humility. Young leaders should be confident in their abilities yet humble enough to recognize their limitations, seek advice, and learn from others. This balance fosters respect and creates an environment where everyone feels valued and empowered to contribute.

Prioritize Ethical Considerations and Social Responsibility

In a world where technology's impact is profound, ethical considerations and social responsibility should be at the forefront of innovation. Young innovators should be guided to think about the broader implications of their work, striving to create solutions that are not only effective but also ethical and beneficial for society.

Develop Resilience and Perseverance

The path of innovation is often fraught with obstacles and setbacks. Developing resilience – the ability to recover from failures and persevere despite difficulties – is crucial. Young leaders should learn that setbacks are a natural part of the innovation process and that persistence often leads to breakthroughs.

Communicate Effectively and Inspire Others

Effective communication is a key leadership skill. Young innovators should learn to articulate their ideas clearly and inspire others with their vision. This involves not only speaking and presenting effectively but also listening actively and empathetically.

Encourage Self-Reflection and Personal Growth

Finally, leadership is as much about personal growth as it is about professional achievement. Young innovators should be encouraged to engage in self-reflection, understand their strengths and weaknesses, and set personal and professional development goals. This holistic approach to leadership fosters well-rounded individuals who are capable of leading with insight and empathy.

Embrace Your Unique Perspective

Teen leaders bring a fresh, often innovative perspective to challenges. It's important to embrace this unique viewpoint, as it can lead to new solutions and approaches. Young leaders should be confident in their ideas and understand that their age is an asset, not a hindrance.

Lead by Example

Leadership is not just about directing others; it's about setting an example. Teen leaders should strive to be role models in their actions and behaviors. This includes showing commitment, integrity, and enthusiasm. Leading by example inspires trust and respect from peers and mentors alike.

Develop Emotional Intelligence

Emotional intelligence is crucial for effective leadership. It involves understanding and managing your own emotions and empathizing with others. Teen leaders should work on developing these skills to enhance their communication, conflict resolution, and team-building abilities.

Foster Inclusivity and Diversity

Good leaders value and promote inclusivity and diversity. Teen leaders should make an effort to understand and appreciate different perspectives and backgrounds. Creating an inclusive environment encourages creativity, collaboration, and a sense of belonging among team members.

Cultivate a Growth Mindset

A growth mindset – the belief that abilities and intelligence can be developed through dedication and hard work – is a powerful tool for teen leaders. It encourages resilience in the face of challenges and a continuous quest for learning and self-improvement.

Practice Effective Communication

Clear and effective communication is fundamental to leadership. Teen leaders should learn to articulate their thoughts clearly and listen actively. Good communication fosters understanding and collaboration, and it's essential for building strong relationships within a team.

Be Open to Feedback and Learning

Feedback is a valuable tool for growth. Young leaders should be open to receiving feedback, both positive and constructive, and use it to improve their skills and approaches. Additionally, they should actively seek opportunities for learning and development.

Prioritize Time Management

Effective time management is a critical skill for leaders. Teen leaders, often balancing school, extracurricular activities, and personal commitments, should learn to prioritize tasks, set goals, and manage their time efficiently.

Build Resilience and Adaptability

Leadership involves navigating uncertainties and setbacks. Developing resilience – the ability to bounce back from challenges – and adaptability – the capacity to adjust to change – is essential for teen leaders. These skills enable them to handle adversity and emerge stronger.

Conclusion

In conclusion, these core principles provide a foundation for teen leadership. By embracing these values and continuously striving to develop their skills, young leaders can make a positive impact in their communities and pave the way for a future of effective and compassionate leadership.

These leadership lessons are intended to guide young innovators as they navigate their own paths. The journey of innovation and leadership is unique for each individual, but these principles provide a foundation for success and fulfillment. My hope is that these lessons inspire the next generation of leaders to pursue their passions, make meaningful contributions, and lead with integrity, creativity, and a vision for a better future.

Chapter 21: Challenges, Resilience, and Perseverance

This section of my journey focuses on the inevitable challenges encountered along the way, and the crucial roles that resilience and perseverance play in overcoming them. These experiences have been integral in shaping my character and approach to both personal and professional obstacles.

Facing Challenges Head-On

Throughout my journey, I've encountered various challenges, ranging from academic pressures to the complexities of managing projects and teams. Each challenge, whether it was a difficult problem in quantum computing or a hurdle in a community service project, required me to confront the situation directly, assess it realistically, and devise a strategy to overcome it.

Learning the Value of Resilience

Resilience has been a key lesson in my growth as a leader and innovator. It's the ability to recover from setbacks, adapt to change, and keep going in the face of adversity. I've learned that resilience isn't just about enduring difficulties; it's about using these experiences as opportunities for learning and personal growth.

Perseverance as a Path to Success

Perseverance has been equally important. The journey of innovation and leadership is rarely smooth or straightforward. Staying committed to my goals, even when progress seemed slow or uncertain, has been essential. I've found that perseverance, coupled with a clear vision, is often what separates successful endeavors from those that fall short.

Overcoming the Fear of Failure

One significant challenge has been overcoming the fear of failure. I've learned to reframe failure not as a setback, but as a natural step in the learning process. Embracing failure as an inevitable part of trying something new or challenging has been crucial in my development as a leader.

Balancing Ambition with Well-being

Another challenge has been balancing ambition with personal well-being. The drive to achieve can sometimes lead to burnout. I've learned the importance of self-care, setting realistic expectations, and understanding that taking breaks and recharging are essential for long-term success.

The Role of Support Systems

I've also learned the importance of having a supportive network. Whether it's family, friends, mentors, or peers, having people who offer encouragement, advice, and a listening ear has been invaluable in navigating challenges.

Continuous Learning from Challenges

Every challenge has been a learning experience. Whether it's developing new skills, gaining deeper insights, or simply learning more about my own strengths and weaknesses, each obstacle has contributed to my personal and professional development.

Future Outlook: Embracing Challenges as Opportunities

Looking ahead, I see challenges not as barriers, but as opportunities to grow, innovate, and lead more effectively. I am committed to maintaining resilience and perseverance in the face of future challenges, using these experiences to become a stronger, more capable leader.

In conclusion, the principles of challenges, resilience, and perseverance are deeply intertwined in my journey. They have taught me invaluable lessons about leadership, personal growth, and the pursuit of goals. Embracing challenges, and learning to overcome them with resilience and perseverance, has been fundamental in shaping my approach to life and leadership.

Chapter 22: College Aspirations and Career Goals

In this chapter, I articulate my aspirations for college and outline the career goals that shape my future. This stage represents a significant transition, where the foundations laid by my past experiences converge with my ambitions, guiding me toward a future rich with potential and purpose.

As I stand at the threshold of a new chapter in my journey, Chapter 11 is about preparing for the next leap forward. This phase involves introspection, strategic planning, and setting new goals, as I anticipate future challenges and opportunities. It's a time of readiness for continued growth, innovation, and impact.

Reflecting on Past Experiences

The first step in preparing for the next phase is to reflect on my past experiences. This involves analyzing both successes and setbacks, understanding what worked and what didn't, and identifying key lessons. Reflection helps to consolidate learning and provides a foundation upon which to build future endeavors.

Setting New Goals and Aspirations

With the insights gained from reflection, I am now setting new goals and aspirations. These objectives are not just career-oriented but also encompass personal development, continued learning, and community impact. Setting clear, achievable goals provides direction and motivation for the journey ahead.

Developing New Skills and Knowledge

In anticipation of future challenges, I am committed to developing new skills and expanding my knowledge base. This may involve formal education, self-study, or practical experiences. Staying abreast of emerging trends in technology, leadership, and social issues is crucial for remaining relevant and effective.

Building and Nurturing Networks

Recognizing the importance of collaboration and support, I am focused on building and nurturing professional and personal networks. These networks provide valuable resources, opportunities for collaboration, and support systems that are essential for growth and success.

Embracing Change and Uncertainty

The future is inherently uncertain, and I am preparing myself to embrace change. This involves being adaptable, open to new ideas, and ready to pivot when necessary. Embracing change also means being prepared to take calculated risks in pursuit of innovation and impact.

Enhancing Leadership and Interpersonal Skills

As I prepare for future leadership roles, enhancing my leadership and interpersonal skills is a priority. This includes honing my abilities in areas such as communication, team management, empathy, and strategic thinking. Effective leadership will be crucial in navigating complex environments and inspiring others.

Prioritizing Health and Well-being

Understanding the demands of an intensive career path, prioritizing health and well-being is more important than ever. This means maintaining a balance between work and personal life, engaging in activities that promote mental and physical health, and ensuring that personal well-being is not overshadowed by professional responsibilities.

Staying Committed to Lifelong Learning

Finally, I remain committed to the principle of lifelong learning. Whether it's through formal education, practical experiences, or personal exploration, continuous learning is the key to personal and professional growth. It keeps me equipped to handle new challenges and seize opportunities that come my way.

Defining College Aspirations

As I look toward college, my aspirations are twofold: to deepen my knowledge in fields that fascinate me, like quantum computing, AI, and robotics, and to expand my horizons in areas that I have yet to explore. I aim to attend a college that not only excels academically but also fosters innovation, critical thinking, and a diverse and inclusive community. My goal is to immerse myself in an environment where I can grow intellectually and personally, engaging with peers and mentors who challenge and inspire me.

Career Goals: Blending Technology and Social Impact

In terms of career goals, I envision a path that seamlessly blends technology with social impact. I am driven by the prospect of working on projects that leverage advanced technologies to address societal challenges. This includes innovations in sustainable energy, educational technology, and healthcare. My aim is to be at the forefront of technological advancements, contributing to solutions that are ethically sound, socially responsible, and globally beneficial.

Pursuing Interdisciplinary Studies

Recognizing the interconnectedness of today's world challenges, I am interested in pursuing interdisciplinary studies. This approach will allow me to integrate knowledge from different fields, such as combining principles of engineering with insights from economics and social sciences, to develop holistic solutions to complex problems.

Gaining Practical Experience through Internships and Research

To complement my academic pursuits, I plan to engage in internships and research opportunities. Gaining practical experience is crucial for applying theoretical knowledge to real-world situations. I aim to work with organizations and research projects that are at the cutting edge of technology and societal development.

Leadership and Entrepreneurial Aspirations

In addition to technical skills, I aspire to hone my leadership and entrepreneurial abilities. I see myself taking on roles that require steering teams, managing projects, and possibly starting ventures that align with my passion for technology and social good.

Lifelong Learning and Personal Development

I am committed to the principle of lifelong learning. Keeping abreast of technological advancements, continually acquiring new skills, and personal development are integral parts of my career goals. This commitment extends beyond formal education to include self-directed learning, attending workshops, and participating in professional networks.

Giving Back through Mentorship and Community Engagement

As I advance in my career, I also aspire to give back to the community. This includes mentoring young enthusiasts in technology and leadership, and engaging in community initiatives that promote STEM education and innovation.

Conclusion

In conclusion, as I prepare for college and delineate my career goals, I am guided by a desire to integrate my passion for technology with a commitment to making a positive impact on society. My aspirations are not just focused on personal achievement but are rooted in a broader vision of contributing to a future where technology and innovation are used for the betterment of all. This chapter is about setting the stage for a journey that is as purposeful as it is ambitious, driven by a continuous quest for knowledge, innovation, and meaningful contribution.

It is about strategically preparing for the next phase of my journey. It's a time of readiness, characterized by reflection, goal-setting, skill development, and a commitment to continuous growth. As I prepare for this next leap, I am fueled by the lessons of the past, the aspirations for the future, and a steadfast commitment to making a positive impact in whatever I pursue.

Final Thoughts: A Message to Fellow Young Leaders

As I conclude this journey, I want to share a message with my fellow young leaders, a reflection of the lessons learned and the insights gained. This message is an amalgamation of encouragement, advice, and a vision for the future, intended to inspire and guide those who are embarking on their own paths of leadership and innovation.

Embrace Your Potential

First and foremost, believe in your potential. You are at the beginning of a remarkable journey filled with opportunities to make a difference. Your age is not a limitation but rather an asset that brings a fresh perspective and innovative ideas to the table.

Cultivate a Vision

Develop a clear vision for what you want to achieve. This vision might evolve over time, but having a sense of direction is crucial. It will guide your decisions, keep you motivated during challenging times, and inspire others to join you in your endeavors.

Value Learning Over Success

Focus on learning and growth rather than just success. Every experience, whether it ends in triumph or failure, is a learning opportunity. Embrace challenges as chances to expand your knowledge and skills.

Lead with Empathy and Integrity

Leadership is as much about empathy and integrity as it is about strategy and execution. Be a leader who listens, understands, and acts with honesty and ethical principles. These qualities build trust and create an environment where everyone feels valued and empowered.

Foster Collaboration

Remember that collaboration is key. Great achievements are rarely the work of one person alone. Seek out mentors, build a supportive team, and engage with your peers. The collective strength of a group can accomplish far more than any individual alone.

Stay Adaptable and Resilient

The world is constantly changing, and adaptability is essential. Stay open to new ideas, be willing to adjust your plans, and learn to navigate through uncertainty. Coupled with resilience, this adaptability will help you overcome obstacles and persist in the face of adversity.

Give Back and Inspire Others

As you progress on your journey, find ways to give back. Mentor others, share your experiences, and contribute to your community. Your journey can be an inspiration to others, sparking a chain reaction of leadership and innovation.

Look After Your Well-being

Lastly, take care of yourself. The pursuit of goals should not come at the expense of your well-being. Balance your ambitions with activities that bring you joy and relaxation. A well-rounded life is not only more sustainable but also more fulfilling.

In Closing

To my fellow young leaders, the future is bright with your presence and potential. Your journeys will undoubtedly be diverse and unique, filled with successes, learning, and growth. Embrace each step with confidence, curiosity, and a commitment to making a positive impact. Remember, the journey of leadership is not just about reaching a destination; it's about the experiences, the people you impact, and the person you become along the way. Keep moving forward, keep dreaming big, and let your journey inspire a world of possibilities.

Epilogue

As I close the pages of this chapter of my life, I stand at the crossroads of reflection and anticipation. This journey, chronicled through the chapters of my experiences, has been more than a mere account of achievements and challenges; it has been a tapestry of growth, learning, and discovery.

Reflection on the Journey

Looking back, I see a path marked by curiosity, driven by a passion for technology and a commitment to making a difference. Each step, whether it involved academic pursuits, leadership roles, or community engagement, was a building block in shaping who I am today. The challenges faced were not just obstacles but opportunities that honed my resilience and broadened my perspective.

Lessons Learned

The journey taught me invaluable lessons. I learned the power of resilience, the importance of empathy in leadership, and the value of a multidisciplinary approach in solving complex problems. It reinforced the notion that true success lies not just in personal achievements but in the impact we have on others and the world.

Gratitude

As I pen down these final thoughts, my heart is filled with gratitude. Gratitude for the mentors who guided me, the peers who journeyed alongside me, and the challenges that molded me. I am thankful for the opportunities I had to learn, to lead, and to serve.

Looking to the Future

The future is a canvas of possibilities. As I step into the next phase of my life, I carry with me the lessons of the past and the hope for the future. My aspirations now extend beyond personal goals to broader ambitions of contributing to societal progress and technological innovation.

A Message to Future Leaders

To those who will walk this path after me, I leave these words: Embrace your journey with open arms. Cherish each experience, for even the smallest moments can have profound impacts. Pursue your passions relentlessly, lead with integrity, and always remember the power of compassion and collaboration.

Reflections on a Path Less Traveled

As I look back on the journey that this book encapsulates, I find myself reflecting on the path less traveled that I chose to embark upon. This path, woven with unique choices and unconventional pursuits, has not only defined my experiences but has also shaped my identity and outlook on life.

The Courage to Choose Differently

Choosing a path less traveled required courage – the courage to step away from the conventional, to embrace uncertainty, and to trust in my own convictions. It was about pursuing passions that were not always mainstream, like diving deep into the realms of quantum computing, AI, and robotics, and integrating these with a strong commitment to social impact.

Challenges as Opportunities

This journey was not without its challenges. Each hurdle, however, was an opportunity to learn, to grow, and to innovate. Whether it was navigating the complexities of advanced technologies, leading teams in uncharted territories, or balancing academic rigor with personal growth, each challenge was a stepping stone towards greater resilience and understanding.

The Value of Interdisciplinary Learning

One of the key realizations from this journey has been the immense value of interdisciplinary learning and thinking. By merging fields like technology, science, and social sciences, I gained a more holistic view of the world's problems and the potential solutions. This approach underscored the importance of looking beyond silos to find integrated, comprehensive solutions.

Impact of Mentorship and Collaboration

Along this path, the impact of mentorship and collaboration has been profound. Engaging with mentors, peers, and professionals from various fields provided invaluable insights and guidance. It highlighted the importance of diverse perspectives and the collective strength that comes from collaboration.

Learning from Failure

Embracing a path less traveled also meant learning to view failure in a new light. Failures were not dead-ends but crucial learning experiences. They taught resilience, adaptability, and the importance of perseverance in the face of adversity.

Prioritizing Balance and Well-being

This journey also taught me the importance of balance – balancing ambition with well-being, professional pursuits with personal interests, and leadership roles with team collaboration. Maintaining this balance was key to sustainable growth and well-being.

Looking Ahead with Optimism

As I reflect on this path less traveled, I look ahead with optimism. The experiences and lessons from this journey have equipped me to face future challenges with confidence and creativity. They reinforce my commitment to continue pursuing a life that blends innovation with impact, intellect with empathy, and ambition with purpose.

A Message to Aspiring Trailblazers

To those contemplating a path less traveled, my message is this: embrace your unique journey with courage and openness. Let your passions guide you, let your values anchor you, and let your vision inspire you. The road less traveled may be challenging, but it is ripe with opportunities for growth, discovery, and fulfillment.

Conclusion

In closing, this journey does not end here; it evolves. It transitions into a new chapter, one filled with unknown adventures, challenges, and triumphs. As I step forward, I do so with the conviction that the experiences chronicled here are just the beginning. The journey continues, and with it, the unwavering quest to make a meaningful difference in the world.

In the end, this is not just my story. It is a testament to the journey of every young individual who dares to dream, to lead, and to make a positive impact in this ever-changing world.

Resources for Young Tech Enthusiasts

As a guide for young individuals with a passion for technology, I have compiled a list of resources that have been instrumental in my journey. These resources, ranging from educational platforms to inspirational materials, are designed to fuel curiosity, provide knowledge, and offer opportunities for growth and engagement in the field of technology.

Online Learning Platforms

1. Coursera - Offers a wide range of courses in computer science, AI, and other tech-related fields.

2. edX - Provides access to courses from universities like MIT and Harvard on topics like data science and engineering.

3. Khan Academy - A great resource for foundational learning in mathematics, science, and computing.

4. Udemy - Features courses on specific tech skills, including coding languages, app development, and more.

Books and Publications

1. "The Innovators" by Walter Isaacson - A historical journey through the digital revolution.

2. "AI Superpowers" by Kai-Fu Lee - Discusses the rise of AI and its implications globally.

3. "How to Create a Mind" by Ray Kurzweil - Explores the future of artificial intelligence and the brain.

4. Popular Science and Wired Magazines - For staying updated on the latest trends and discoveries in technology.

Websites and Online Resources

1. MIT Technology Review - Provides insights into the latest technological innovations and trends.

2. TechCrunch - A leading source for tech news and analysis.

3. Stack Overflow - A community of developers answering questions and sharing coding knowledge.

4. IEEE Spectrum - Offers in-depth coverage of engineering and applied sciences.

Youth Programs and Competitions

1. Google Science Fair - An online competition open to students aged 13-18 to share their science projects.

2. FIRST Robotics Competition - An international high school robotics competition.

3. Intel International Science and Engineering Fair - A global science competition for high school students.

4. NASA's Internship Programs - Offers students a chance to work on cutting-edge research.

Podcasts and YouTube Channels

1. TED Talks Technology - Features presentations on technology and innovation.

2. CodeNewbie - A podcast for those new to coding.

3. The Vergecast - Discusses the week in tech news.

4. Computerphile (YouTube) - Explains various computer science concepts in an accessible manner.

Networking and Community Involvement

1. Meetup.com - Find local tech groups and meetups.

2. GitHub - Join projects and contribute to open-source software.

3. LinkedIn Groups - Network with professionals and join technology-focused groups.

4. Hackathons - Participate in local or online hackathons to gain hands-on experience and meet like-minded peers.

Conclusion

These resources are just a starting point for young tech enthusiasts. The key is to explore, experiment, and find what ignites your passion within the vast and exciting field of technology. Stay curious, keep learning, and use these tools to carve out your own path in the tech world.

Recommended Reading

For young leaders looking to grow and develop their skills, knowledge, and perspectives, a well-chosen selection of books can be incredibly valuable. The following list of recommended readings covers various aspects of leadership, personal development, and influential thinking. These books provide insights and inspiration essential for any aspiring leader's journey.

1. "Leaders Eat Last" by Simon Sinek

• Explores the concept of servant leadership and the importance of leaders in creating a safe, trusting environment for their teams.

2. "The 7 Habits of Highly Effective People" by Stephen R. Covey

• A classic in personal and professional effectiveness, offering a principle-centered approach for solving personal and professional problems.

3. "Mindset: The New Psychology of Success" by Carol S. Dweck

• Discusses the growth mindset, a perspective that challenges and abilities can be developed through dedication and hard work.

4. "Dare to Lead: Brave Work. Tough Conversations. Whole Hearts." by Brené Brown

• Focuses on developing courage and building resilient and empathetic leadership, emphasizing the power of vulnerability.

5. "Start with Why: How Great Leaders Inspire Everyone to Take Action" by Simon Sinek

• Explores the importance of understanding the 'why' behind actions and decisions, crucial for inspiring and leading effectively.

6. "Drive: The Surprising Truth About What Motivates Us" by Daniel H. Pink

• Investigates the core aspects of motivation and how they can be harnessed to enhance personal and team productivity.

7. "How to Win Friends and Influence People" by Dale Carnegie

• A timeless guide on effective communication and interpersonal skills, vital for any leader.

8. "Good to Great: Why Some Companies Make the Leap and Others Don't" by Jim Collins

• Provides insights into what differentiates top-performing companies from the rest, focusing on leadership strategies and organizational culture.

9. "The Lean Startup: How Today's Entrepreneurs Use Continuous Innovation to Create Radically Successful Businesses" by Eric Ries

• Offers a new approach for startups and innovation, emphasizing the importance of adaptable and agile business practices.

Conclusion

These books are more than just sources of information; they are tools for introspection, inspiration, and transformation. They challenge young leaders to think differently, act with purpose, and lead with integrity. Whether you're just starting on your leadership journey or looking to enhance your skills, these readings offer a wealth of knowledge and guidance to help you navigate the path ahead.

Acknowledgments

As I reflect upon the journey encapsulated in this book, I am filled with profound gratitude for the myriad of influences that have shaped my path. It is with great appreciation that I extend my acknowledgments, including a special note for the honors and awards that have recognized my efforts.

Family

To my family, whose unwavering love and support have been my foundation. Your sacrifices and belief in my abilities have been the cornerstones of my successes. For every late night, every word of encouragement, and every moment of understanding, I am eternally grateful.

Mentors and Educators

A heartfelt thanks to my mentors and educators, whose wisdom has been a guiding light. Your commitment to nurturing my potential, challenging my thinking, and fostering a spirit of inquiry has been invaluable in shaping not just my intellect but also my character.

Peers and Team Members

To my peers and team members, with whom I've shared countless hours of collaboration and learning. Your companionship and shared enthusiasm for our projects have made our successes even more rewarding.

Community and Volunteer Organizations

I am deeply grateful to the community and volunteer organizations, particularly FEMA, for providing opportunities to serve and make a tangible difference. These experiences have been instrumental in my personal and professional growth.

Awards and Honors

Special acknowledgment is due to the prestigious awards and recognitions that have honored my efforts:

• The US Congressional Award, a testament to civic engagement, personal development, and dedication to service. This honor stands as a symbol of my commitment to community and leadership.

• The Presidential Volunteer Service Award – a recognition of my dedication to volunteerism and impact on the community.

• The American Citizenship Award, which recognized my contributions to promoting citizenship and community welfare.

These accolades have not only been honors but also motivators, encouraging me to continue striving for excellence and making a positive impact.

Publishers and Editorial Team

My gratitude extends to the publishers and editorial team for your expertise and dedication in bringing my story to life. Your commitment to authenticity and detail has been crucial in crafting a book that resonates with my journey.

Friends and Well-wishers

To my friends and well-wishers, your support and joy in my achievements have been a source of great comfort and encouragement. Your presence has been a reminder of the importance of balance and happiness in life's journey.

Conclusion

In conclusion, this journey, documented in these pages, is not just a tale of personal achievement but a tapestry woven with the contributions of each individual and institution mentioned, and many unmentioned. Your roles in my life have been chapters in themselves, and for this, I am forever thankful. As I embark on future endeavors, I carry with me the lessons learned, the memories cherished, and a deep sense of gratitude for every element that has been part of this extraordinary journey. Thank you.

Sincerely,

Rohan Jay

Notes

Printed in Great Britain
by Amazon